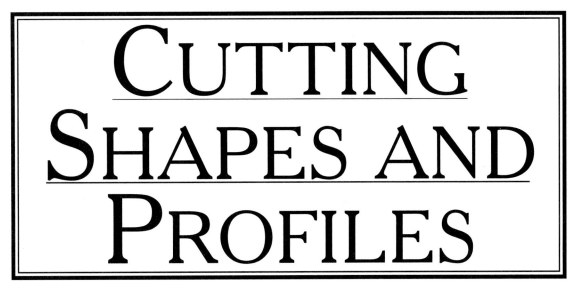

MASTERING WOODWORKING™

CUTTING
SHAPES AND
PROFILES

MASTERING WOODWORKING™

CUTTING SHAPES AND PROFILES

Techniques, Tips, and Problem-Solving Tricks

MARK DUGINSKE
Author of the best-selling *Band Saw Handbook*

with JOHN KELSEY

Rodale Press, Inc.
Emmaus, Pennsylvania

OUR MISSION

We publish books that empower people's lives.

RODALE BOOKS

The authors and editors who compiled this book have tried to make all of the contents as accurate and as correct as possible. Plans, illustrations, photographs, and text have all been carefully checked and cross-checked. However, due to the variability of local conditions, construction materials, personal skill, and so on, neither the authors nor Rodale Press assumes any responsibility for any injuries suffered or for damages or other losses incurred that result from the material presented herein. All instructions and plans should be carefully studied and clearly understood before beginning construction.

Printed in the United States of America on acid-free ∞, recycled ♺ paper

Mastering Woodworking: Cutting Shapes and Profiles Editorial Staff

Editors: Ken Burton, Tony O'Malley
Book Designer: Jan Melchior
Interior Illustrators: Glenn Hughes, Frank Rohrbach
Interior Photographers: Robert Gerheart, John Hamel, Mitch Mandel, Kurt Wilson
Interior Photo Stylist: Pam Simpson
Cover Photographer: John Hamel
Technical Artist: Dale Mack
Copy Editor: Nancy N. Bailey, Elizabeth Barone
Manufacturing Coordinator: Melinda B. Rizzo
Indexer: Nan N. Badgett
Editorial Assistance: Sue Nickol and Lori Schaffer
Project Designers:
   Ken Burton: Folding Screen
   Tony O'Malley: Accent Lamp, Frame-and-Panel Nightstand, and Classical Bookcase

On the cover: Cove cutting on the table saw (page 64)

Rodale Home and Garden Books

Vice President and Editorial Director:
   Margaret Lydic Balitas
Managing Editor, Woodworking and DIY Books: Kevin Ireland
Associate Art Director: Mary Ellen Fanelli
Studio Manager: Leslie Keefe
Copy Director: Dolores Plikaitis
Production Manager: Helen Clogston
Office Manager: Karen Earl-Braymer
Rodale Press Design Shop staff:
   Phil Gehret and Fred Matlack

Accessories in project photos supplied by Geiser's Furniture, Bethlehem, Pa.; Interior Ideas, Allentown, Pa.; Crest Wholesale Carpet distributors, Allentown, Pa.; and Royal Furniture, Emmaus, Pa.

Photo on page 81 by JET Equipment and Tools. Photo on page 77 by Delta International Machinery Corporation. Photo on page 87 by C.S. Onsrud, Inc.

If you have any questions or comments concerning this book, please write to:
   Rodale Press, Inc.
   Book Readers' Service
   33 East Minor Street
   Emmaus, PA 18098

Library of Congress Cataloging-in-Publication Data

Duginske, Mark
   Mastering woodworking. Cutting shapes and profiles / Mark Duginske with
John Kelsey.
      p.   cm. – (Mastering woodworking)
   Includes index.
   ISBN 0–87596–746–9 (hardcover : alk. paper)
   1. Woodwork. 2. Wood–cutting tools. 3. Routers (Tools)
  I. Kelsey, John, date. II. Title. III. Series.
TT185.D79 1996
684'. 08–dc20   96–20300

Distributed in the book trade by St. Martin's Press

2 4 6 8 10 9 7 5 3 1   hardcover

ABOUT MARK DUGINSKE AND JOHN KELSEY

While Mark Duginske is currently occupied as a writer, inventor, and woodworker, he also has worked as a registered nurse. He has developed many innovative products for woodworking, including Cool Blocks band-saw-blade guides. A master of the band saw, he demonstrates his techniques at seminars and conventions across the country. He is also the author of four books on woodworking, including the *Band Saw Handbook* and *Mastering Woodworking Machines*. Duginske lives in Merrill, Wisconsin.

Coauthor John Kelsey is a journalist and amateur woodworker. From 1976 until 1984, he was the editor of *Fine Woodworking* magazine. He has edited many books and writes frequently about woodworking and furniture design. In 1994, Kelsey founded Cambium Press, an independent publishing company specializing in the practical and decorative arts. He lives in Newtown, Connecticut.

CONTENTS

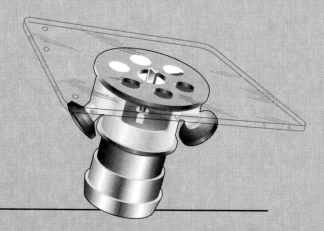

Projects

INTRODUCTION

Before you can build something out of wood, you've got to turn rough planks into straight, flat boards. It's the prerequisite for all joint making. Once the joints are cut, though, the process takes an about-face of sorts, when you find yourself tampering with the straight lines and flat surfaces by adding shape, contour, and subtle details to the wood.

For me, shaping wood has always been the most enjoyable part of the woodworking process. For one thing, it's full of pleasant surprises and experimentation. When routing a profile into a table edge, for example, I always take a series of light passes, gauging the look of the edge after each pass. Sometimes I stop before reaching the depth of cut intended because I like what I see before I get to it. Another great thing about shaping is that it involves creative choices. That means the rules are flexible and I can test ideas as I work my way through a project. For instance, while laying out a shape, I may discover a way to enhance it by adding a second profile using a different router bit.

Shaping also brings out unexpected changes in the grain of the wood. An oval tabletop, an arched rail, a cabriole leg—all these shapes are one thing drawn on paper, but when you cut them into a piece of wood, the beauty of the material shines forth in ways that are never fully predictable because each piece of wood is unique.

The techniques and projects in this book will help you explore all the potential of shaping so you can put your own creative stamp on the pieces you build. It presents every shaping process—from chamfering the edge of a table with a hand plane, to sawing and spokeshaving the surfaces of a cabriole leg—in a step-by-step format. Color illustrations and photographs walk you through each technique in a no-nonsense way. You'll see that shaping techniques are no more difficult than the planing and joint-making processes that precede them. And you'll learn how to make complex shapes using tools you probably already have.

Cutting Shapes and Profiles starts out with a brief look at the basic vocabulary of shapes and profiles and shows how every profile imaginable can be reduced to a few basic shapes that have been used for millennia. Next, author Mark Duginske shows how you can build a router table, buy a few basic bits, and make your router the most versatile shaping tool in your shop. Though the router is often the tool of choice for shaping, this book also explains how to use the band saw, table saw, drill press, lathe, and assorted hand tools for cutting shapes and profiles.

At every turn, Duginske shows you how to make clever jigs that turn potentially difficult techniques into simple ones. Plus, he applies his jigs and techniques to real things you'll want to make—a gooseneck molding in the chapter on shaping curved edges and an arch-top door in the chapter on raised-panel shaping.

Throughout the book, you'll find these added features:

- Troubleshooting boxes that point out potential pitfalls and how to avoid them
- Problem Solving boxes that help get you out of many of the most common woes
- Rippings boxes that offer helpful tips and tricks
- Fact or Fiction boxes that debunk common misconceptions about woodworking techniques

Finally, there are four projects at the back of the book designed specifically to make use of the techniques discussed up front. Try the techniques there, or apply them to your own projects. Either way, I think you'll find that shaping can take a project on a turn you hadn't planned and that keeps woodworking fun.

Tony O'Malley

TECHNIQUES

1

An Introduction to Cutting Shapes and Profiles

Key Ingredients

Shaping and profiling wood means removing what you don't want in order to reveal what you do want. Think of it as a subtractive process—wood can't be molded like plastic or clay, so it has to be cut into the desired form.

Tools for Shaping

There are a large number of tools and machines for cutting away this excess wood, ranging from whittling knives and carving gouges to high-powered industrial shapers. Today, however, the technology of choice for the home shop woodworker is the electric router, which can shape edges, raise panels, cut precise circles, duplicate patterns, and do much more.

However, even woodworkers with a fully tricked-out router table and a drawer full of bits often find that many shaping and profiling operations can be done more easily with other tools or with a combination of the router and other tools.

The cabinet shown in *A Compendium of Shapes* illustrates how a single piece of furniture can require a wide range of shaping

tools and techniques. Below is a list of the tools that are most practical for small shop woodworking, along with a description of their best uses:

- A band saw is the best tool for sawing curved shapes, particularly complex curves like cabriole legs and curves through thick stock like a chair back. It won't produce finished results by itself, but it removes excess wood so you can complete the job more quickly with other shaping tools. A saber saw does similar work but it's portable--and if you're just starting out, it's a lot cheaper than a band saw.

- Though the table saw primarily cuts straight and true, it also can be a useful shaping machine. With a fence clamped at an angle to the blade, you can cut large cove moldings. With a molding head attached, you can cut shapes into the face or edge of boards or panels. In fact, because the wood lies flat on the table saw, the molding head is the safest and most accurate tool for cutting flutes or beads into wide stock for things like architectural moldings and fluted pilasters. A molding head on a radial-arm saw gives you a setup more akin to a shaper. The table saw also cuts rabbets and grooves when they're part of more shapely profiles, and it removes waste so router bits have less wood to eat through.

- Sanders can shape wood as well as smooth it after it's been shaped. A disc sander can aggressively true up convex forms—circular discs cut on the band saw, for example. A drum sander mounted on the drill press is an efficient setup for smoothing concave curves, such as table aprons and curved door rails, right off the band saw.

- Hand tools impart fine details that machines cannot. Planes, spokeshaves, rasps and files, chisels and gouges—all these tools allow you to add the subtle and distinguishing touch of handwork to your woodworking. The scratch stock is a tool you can quickly make yourself to cut small profiles, such as a bead around the edge of a drawer or door. It's a pleasant relief from the whine of a router.

- The shaper is the workhorse of commercial cabinet and mill-work shops. While a router table is a good substitute for light- to medium-duty work, you can't beat a shaper for pro-duction work such as making a kitchen's worth of frame-and-panel doors. Finally, the shaper excels at cutting large profiles like hand rails and crown mold-ing. With router bits, these shapes often require a combina-tion of several bits, while on the shaper, a single cutter can do the job.

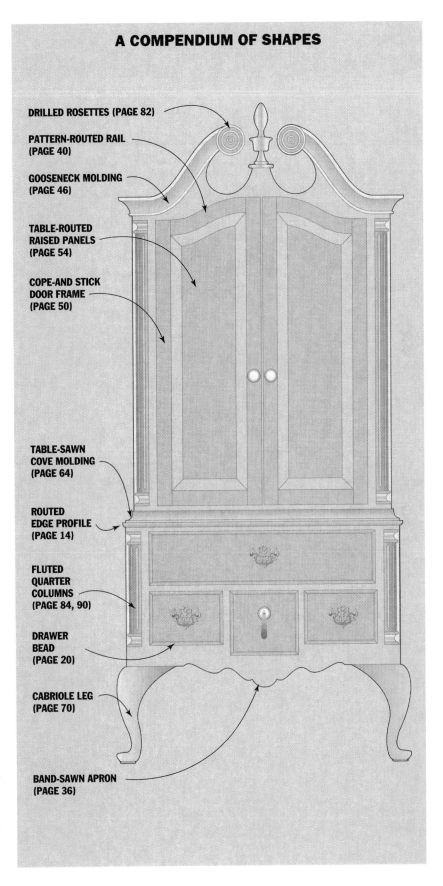

A COMPENDIUM OF SHAPES

DRILLED ROSETTES (PAGE 82)

PATTERN-ROUTED RAIL (PAGE 40)

GOOSENECK MOLDING (PAGE 46)

TABLE-ROUTED RAISED PANELS (PAGE 54)

COPE-AND-STICK DOOR FRAME (PAGE 50)

TABLE-SAWN COVE MOLDING (PAGE 64)

ROUTED EDGE PROFILE (PAGE 14)

FLUTED QUARTER COLUMNS (PAGE 84, 90)

DRAWER BEAD (PAGE 20)

CABRIOLE LEG (PAGE 70)

BAND-SAWN APRON (PAGE 36)

How Moldings Work

Often it is the specific shape of the moldings and profiles that distinguishes one style of furniture from the next. If you want to elevate your woodworking beyond simply rounding over every edge, it will pay to develop an understanding of what moldings do as well as how to make them.

The first thing to realize is that all furniture and architectural moldings are composed of a few basic geometric shapes, which have been handed down to us from ancient times. You can vary the size of these elements, or you can vary the way they go together, but you won't have much luck trying to invent new ones. There aren't any.

This doesn't mean you can't be creative in your choice of molding profiles. Although the basic vocabulary has only a handful of words, they can go together in infinite ways.

Function First

Moldings ease the transition and fill the gaps between adjacent surfaces. Consider architectural room trim. Base moldings bridge the junction between the floor and the wall. Crown moldings do the same at the ceiling. Their function is to conceal gaps and irregularities in the joints of the building. You could get the job done with meager strips of quarter-round molding, but then the molding's function would be obvious, calling attention to the minor construction defects it's supposed to hide.

Instead, these moldings give you the opportunity to add visual interest at the same time. There are moldings of all shapes and sizes for every architectural style, and their design satisfies both function and aesthetics. This is why architectural moldings usually are assembled from several pieces. It's not that you couldn't cut the whole profile in one board (though sometimes that's also true). It's that you need the little bead or quarter round as a separate piece of wood, so it can bend right along with the irregularities in the wall and floor. This is illus-

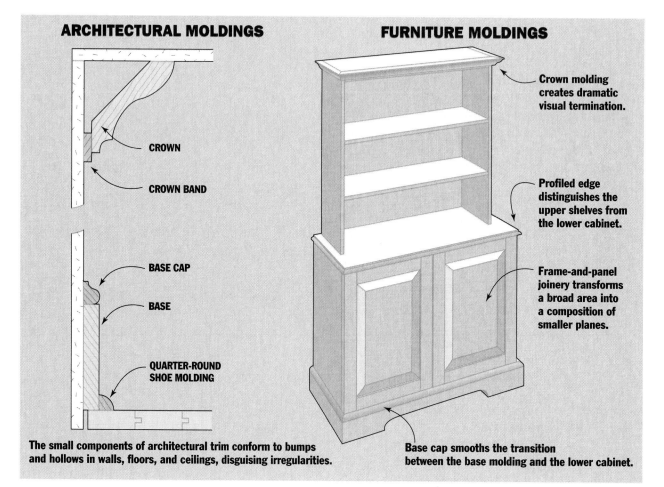

ARCHITECTURAL MOLDINGS

CROWN

CROWN BAND

BASE CAP

BASE

QUARTER-ROUND
SHOE MOLDING

The small components of architectural trim conform to bumps and hollows in walls, floors, and ceilings, disguising irregularities.

FURNITURE MOLDINGS

Crown molding creates dramatic visual termination.

Profiled edge distinguishes the upper shelves from the lower cabinet.

Frame-and-panel joinery transforms a broad area into a composition of smaller planes.

Base cap smooths the transition between the base molding and the lower cabinet.

A VOCABULARY OF SHAPES

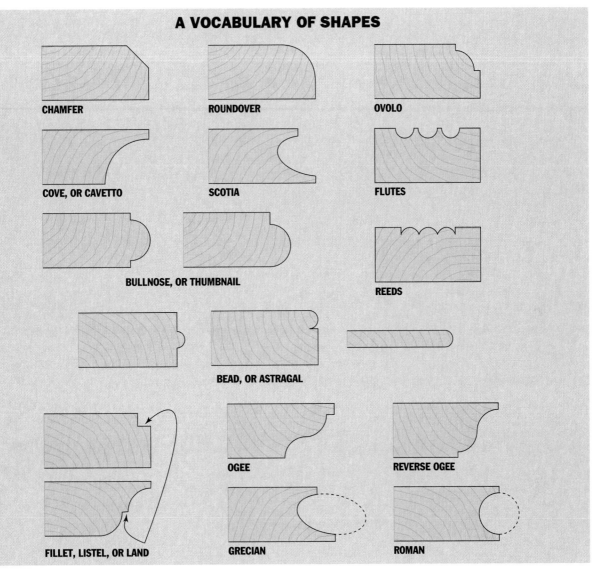

CHAMFER

ROUNDOVER

OVOLO

COVE, OR CAVETTO

SCOTIA

FLUTES

BULLNOSE, OR THUMBNAIL

REEDS

BEAD, OR ASTRAGAL

FILLET, LISTEL, OR LAND

OGEE

REVERSE OGEE

GRECIAN

ROMAN

trated in *Architectural Moldings.*

In furniture making, moldings serve the same function of easing the transition between surfaces. But as in architecture, moldings also play an important aesthetic role. For example, the crown molding shown in *Furniture Moldings* creates a decisive visual termination; it defines precisely where the top of the hutch ends. It also defines the space the hutch occupies more boldly than if the cabinet had a plain, square-edged top. This may seem obvious, but cover the crown molding with a piece of paper and

note the dramatic difference. Moldings also help define the individual elements within the composition of a piece of furniture. The beveled panel and the bead around the inside edge of the frame on a raised-panel door both serve this function.

The Basic Vocabulary of Shapes

Starting with a square edge, you can knock off the corner, or arris, to create a chamfer, or round the edge to make a roundover. You can cut a concave hollow, either cove or scotia, or you can make its inverse, a

convex bead, either bullnose or ovolo. Small beads right next to one another are called reeds; small coves close together are flutes. You can combine an innie and an outie to make an S-curve, either ogee or reverse ogee. You can make a little flat, called a land, listel, or fillet, to join one shape to another. When the beads and coves are oval or elliptical in section, the molding is said to be Grecian. When they are circular in section, the molding is said to be Roman. This is the basic lineup of moldings, as illustrated in *A Vocabulary of Shapes.*

Working with Routers

Of all the tools you can use for shaping and molding wood, the router is the most versatile. You can attach router bits and cutters that do just about every woodworking operation, from raising panels and cutting deep mortises to shaping ornate moldings and forming perfect circles and ellipses. Still, a router isn't much more than an electric motor with handles, a flat baseplate, and a means of holding a bit on the shaft. It's the way you use it that really makes the difference. Shaping edges is just the beginning of a router's domain. Attach a trammel to a router fitted

Laminate trimmer (left), 1½-horsepower fixed-base router (middle left), 3-horsepower heavy-duty router with speed control (middle right), and plunge router (right) form the basic lineup of routers. If you only buy one, choose a 1½-horsepower fixed-base router.

RIPPINGS

GETTING THE MOST FROM A SINGLE ROUTER

Several companies offer a tool with a 3½-inch-diameter motor as their basic router. Buy one of these with its accompanying fixed base, then get a plunge base from Porter Cable, which they make to accommodate their 3½-inch-diameter routers. This combination will give you a lot of versatility without having to spend a lot of money.

This plunge router base fits many 3½-inch models, giving you plunge-routing capability for less than half the cost of a separate plunge router.

with a straight bit, and you can cut perfect circles. Turn a router upside down and attach it to a table, and you increase its versatility tenfold. In effect, you've got yourself a small shaper.

Router Types

There are three types of routers: general-purpose fixed-base routers, plunge routers, and laminate trimmers, as shown in the photo above. If you spend a lot of time at woodworking, you'll eventually have one of each. But, with a few exceptions, you can do most shaping operations using a 1½-horsepower, fixed-base router. It should be a professional grade tool made by a company like Bosch, DeWalt, Hitachi, or Porter Cable, to name a few. And it should have both ¼- and ½-inch collets so you can use the full range of bits and cutters. A tool like this will work fine in a router table, too.

The only notable limit to shaping with a router of this caliber is when you try to use extra large specialty bits like cope-and-stick cutters and panel raisers. For these, you need more power and a slower speed. You can get both features in a larger router—3 horsepower or more—with speed control, but you'll pay twice as much for it. And you wouldn't want one of those behemoths as your only router. They're simply too bulky for general hand-routing operations. On the other hand, a large router with speed control is your best bet for use in a router table, but only if you can afford to dedicate a router to that purpose.

Laminate trimmers do more than trim laminate. These little routers are powerful enough to trim solid wood edge banding and to cut small profiles in hardwood edges. They're excellent for one-handed use, such as when you rout a circle with a trammel and need a free hand to reposition the power cord so you can complete the cut. And they're perfect for delicate operations, like routing tiny grooves for inlay or mortises for small hardware.

Finally, plunge routers are a recent innovation designed for routing mortises and other stopped cuts. You can use a plunge router to cut shapes, but the height adjustment mechanism is spring-loaded and can't be fine-tuned the way a fixed-base router can. Some models offer a fine-depth adjustment as an accessory, but the range of adjustment is still limited. Unless you buy an after-market height-adjustment mechaniasm, a plunge router is not suitable for a router table.

TROUBLESHOOTING

TIGHTENING THE COLLET

There are three common mistakes that can lead to poor cutting action by a router. They may even damage the collet, as shown in the drawing.

● Don't tighten the collet nut with the shank of the bit bottomed out in the collet. Tightening the collet draws the shank slightly-down into the opening. If the shank bottoms out, the tightening action will force the shank back out of the tightened collet, scoring the inside of the collet along the way. A scored collet can't grip shanks securely. The bit may be cocked off center, it might vibrate, and it might drop out.

● Be sure that at least two-thirds of the shank's length is in the collet. Any less and the bit will vibrate or may be ejected from the collet during heavy cuts.

● Many cutters have a fillet where the shank meets the bit, as shown in the drawing. Tightening the collet against the fillet will prevent a firm grip. Be sure you pull the bit out $\frac{1}{16}$ of an inch or so beyond the fillet before tightening.

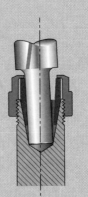

Bit is bottomed out. Tightening the nut will cock the bit off-center.

Two-thirds of the shank should be in the collet.

Too little of the shank is in the collet. Vibration is likely and the bit could be ejected.

Collet grips the fillet. The shank won't be fully locked in the collet.

Router Bits and Cutters

You can spend a lot of money on router bits and cutters, but the truth is, you don't have to. I get plenty of mileage out of a few basic bits and cutters, which I combine to make the shapes I need. I don't buy a special bit until I'm sure I'll need to use it over and over again.

Straight Bits

Straight bits are essential for reproducing shapes from patterns and for routing circles or ellipses with a trammel. They come with straight flutes or spiral flutes, which are better because their shearing cut leaves the wood smoother. Spiral-fluted straight cutters made of high-speed steel are similar to machinists' end mills. Both are very efficient and leave an exceptionally smooth surface.

A pilot bearing on a straight bit allows it to follow a straight or curved edge or template. When the bit and pilot bearing are the same diameter, it's called a flush-trim bit. The pilot can be mounted at either end of the cutting edge, as shown in *Straight*

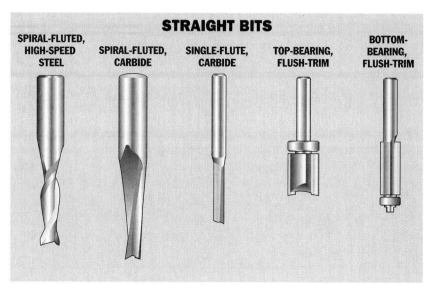

STRAIGHT BITS

SPIRAL-FLUTED, HIGH-SPEED STEEL | SPIRAL-FLUTED, CARBIDE | SINGLE-FLUTE, CARBIDE | TOP-BEARING, FLUSH-TRIM | BOTTOM-BEARING, FLUSH-TRIM

Bits. When mounted at the far end opposite the shank, it's called a bottom-bearing bit. This is the more common arrangement. When mounted on the shank nearest the router motor, it's

RIPPINGS

SAVING SAMPLES

Whenever you rout with a new bit or cutter or use one to cut a new shape, make a sample molding and stash it. Soon you'll have dozens of samples that can help you solve construction and design problems before you turn the router on.

called a top-bearing or pattern-following bit. It's well worth having at least one of each.

Some cutters have removable bearings, and some can be fitted with larger or smaller bearings to make a rabbet or a shaped cut a fixed distance away from a pattern. These are useful for making matched positive and negative shapes, such as for inlay.

Groove-Forming Bits

Groove-forming router bits like those shown in *Groove Formers* have no pilot bearing. This allows them to make a shaped groove in the middle of a board. Groove for-

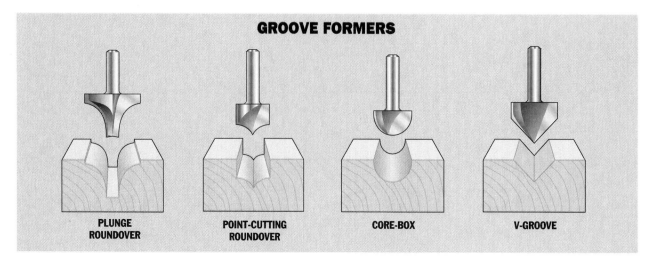

GROOVE FORMERS

PLUNGE ROUNDOVER | POINT-CUTTING ROUNDOVER | CORE-BOX | V-GROOVE

mers can also be used to shape all or part of an edge. Since they don't have a pilot bearing, you must work with a fence or a guide bushing.

Groove formers are easy to combine to rout complex profiles. Core-box, V-groove, and roundover profiles are useful in smaller sizes for making furniture and cabinets and in larger sizes for making architectural trim.

Edge-Forming Bits

Edge formers, which usually have pilot bearings, are for shaping all or part of the edge of a piece of wood. (See *Edge Formers.*) The bearing follows the edge of the wood and limits the depth of the cut, though you can always make a shallower cut by using a fence. Avoid cutters with nonrotating steel pilots. They'll often burn the edge of your work-

piece, especially in wood with heat-sensitive pitch, like cherry.

Special Purpose Bits

For every wood-shaping situation, some enterprising fellow has

devised a special-purpose router cutter. Most of them are ingenious, sometimes useful, but typically expensive. Watch out for large-diameter bits. When the diameter gets over about 2 inches, you need a router with electronic speed control so you can run the bit at a reduced speed.

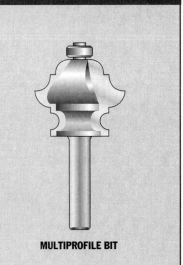
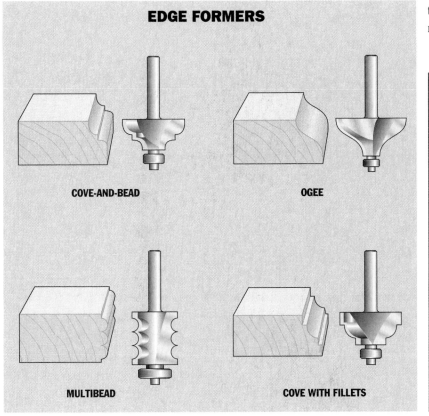

EDGE FORMERS

COVE-AND-BEAD

OGEE

MULTIBEAD

COVE WITH FILLETS

Router Tables

A router table turns a small portable tool into a stationary shaping machine. Moving the wood past the router is often better than moving the router over the wood. First, the table allows you to set up fences, hold-downs, and guards, so that most operations become safer and more accurate. Second, you can rout long, narrow stock that would be impossible to do with a hand-held router. And third, a router table lets you use an array of bits designed specifically for the router table— panel raisers and cope-and-stick sets, for example.

A good router table is the only woodworking machine you can easily build yourself. It doesn't have to be elaborate to do a good job, but there are a few variables to consider before building your own.

Router Table Options

A freestanding router table, like the one in the photo above right, is always ready to use. But like your jointer and table saw, it's always occupying floor space. A bench-top table has to be set up every time you need it—see the photo below at right. It's also taller than the free-standing router table—an advantage for small work, but a disadvantage for large work. I prefer the cantilevered alternative shown in the photo on the opposite page (top).

A cabinet base under a router table adds stabilizing mass, muffles the motor noise, and offers a place to store cutters and accessories. However, it can fill up with chips, make changing cutters more difficult, and prevent heat from dissipating, harming the motor. If

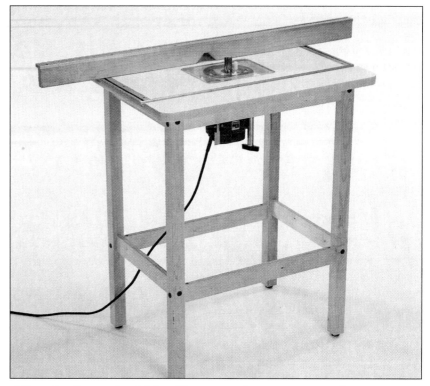

A freestanding router table with an open frame, such as this commercial model, is easy to sweep around, and it's light enough to move when necessary.

This bench-top router table can be built quickly and is very effective to use. (See plans on page 12.) It's made from ¾-inch plywood, and the top has plastic laminate on both the top and bottom surfaces.

you make a base cabinet, leave the router compartment open at the back for ventilation.

No matter what type of router table you make, the best way to mount the router is shown in *Putting the Router into the Tabletop* on page 12. The first step is to replace the factory baseplate with an oversized rectangular base of

Lexan or a similar plastic. You can buy a ready-made baseplate, or buy the plastic and cut and drill it yourself. The baseplate then rests on six leveling pins. This way you can lift the router and base out of the table to change bits, or use it for a free-hand routing operation without any fuss.

A bare-bones router table is all you really need for many shaping operations, but the more you use it, the more you'll want to add some accessories that make it even easier and safer to use. These include a lift-up hinged top so you can change bits without bending over or removing the router, rubber hold-down wheels that hold the stock tight to the table and fence and prevent kickbacks, and a miter gauge slot for making end-grain cuts. The one accessory I wouldn't want to work without is an electrical foot switch. This device allows you to turn the router on and off with your toe, so you don't have to reach under the table and fumble around for the switch. It makes every operation safer. Most models have a double outlet, so your shop vacuum can go on whenever the router does.

If you have a pillar in your shop or access to the building's studs, this kind of setup may be a good choice. The cantilevered 2 X 10s are anchored permanently to the post, but the router table is removable. When I'm not routing, I use it as a chop-saw station.

RIPPINGS

TWO ARE BETTER THAN ONE

Once you've made a good router table and done some work with it, you're likely to decide to make a second one. That way, you can move efficiently between two setups. You can leave one router set for a cut you know you'll return to, while you work on with the other. Or you can set them up to make a two-cut sequence.

An old kitchen cabinet makes a serviceable router table base. The open back provides ventilation.

SHOP SOLUTIONS: Bench-Top Router Table

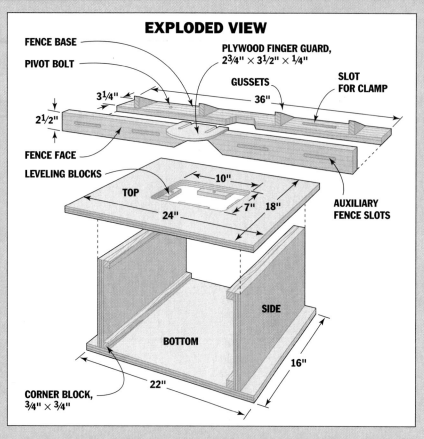

EXPLODED VIEW

FENCE BASE

PIVOT BOLT

PLYWOOD FINGER GUARD,
2¾" × 3½" × ¼"

GUSSETS

SLOT FOR CLAMP

3¼"

36"

2½"

FENCE FACE

LEVELING BLOCKS

TOP

10"

7" 18"

24"

AUXILIARY FENCE SLOTS

SIDE

BOTTOM

16"

CORNER BLOCK,
¾" × ¾"

22"

The router table shown here in the *Exploded View* (and in the bottom photo on page 10) is simple to construct, yet versatile. The open frame construction makes it easy to install and adjust the router, and the chips won't collect around the motor, so it won't overheat. The bottom panel provides a surface for clamping the table to your bench top. The dimensions given in the drawing accommodate mid-sized routers such as the Porter-Cable 690. Make sure the side panels are tall enough for the router you intend to use.

I always center the cutout in the top of the table, but there are advantages to having it off-set. You can work closer to the front edge for typical edge rout-

STEP BY STEP: PUTTING THE ROUTER INTO THE TABLETOP

STEP 1 Position the router's baseplate where you want it on the top. Trace around the baseplate, and drill holes at the corners of your layout.

STEP 2 Cut out the waste with a saber saw. Cut inside the lines slightly, so you can rout the waste off cleanly.

ing, then work on the back side when you need a broader support surface. Choose which will work best for you.

You can make the fence and simply clamp it to the table, or you can use the pivot method shown in the *Exploded View*. The left end of the fence is bolted to the tabletop. With the bolt as a pivot, you adjust the right end of the fence and need only one clamp to lock it in place. I routed a slot through the base of the fence for a quick-grip clamp—the clamp is free to move forward and back, but it's trapped in the slot and is always there when I need it. I also routed slots in the face of the fence. These accommodate the adjustable split-fence system shown in "Shaping the Whole Edge" on page 22.

To make the router table, follow these steps:

STEP 1 Saw the plywood parts to finished size. Cut the corner blocks from straight, clear wood, and pre-drill the screw holes.

STEP 2 Make the router cutout before you assemble the table, following the steps shown in "Putting the Router into the Tabletop."

STEP 3 Glue and screw the corner blocks onto the side panels. Clamp and screw the sides to the bottom and top.

STEP 4 Make the fence from straight hardwood. Or, if you used a high-quality, void-free plywood for the bottom, you can make the fence from that. The extra length allows you to clamp supports for long stock, as shown on page 31. Glue and clamp the

fence face to the fence base, and add a pair of plywood gussets on each side of center to make sure the fence is square. If you use screws, make sure they are completely countersunk into the face of the fence.

STEP 5 To add the pivoting feature to the fence, drill a $\frac{3}{8}$-inch hole at one end of the fence base for the pivot bolt—it must be snug to the bolt so there is no play. Rout a $\frac{5}{16}$-inch slot into the other end, as shown in the *Exploded View*. The slot makes it easier to clamp the fence and keeps the clamp attached to the fence.

To add auxiliary fences to the main fence, drill four $\frac{5}{16}$-inch slots centered in the face of the main fence, as shown. When you make an auxiliary fence, just line up the bolt holes with the slots.

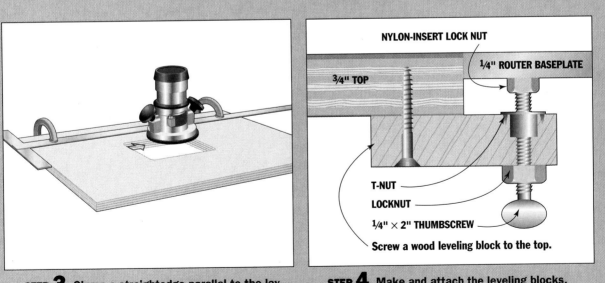

NYLON-INSERT LOCK NUT

$\frac{1}{4}$" ROUTER BASEPLATE

$\frac{3}{4}$" TOP

T-NUT

LOCKNUT

$\frac{1}{4}$" × 2" THUMBSCREW

Screw a wood leveling block to the top.

STEP 3 Clamp a straightedge parallel to the layout lines, and rout the four edges of the cutout clean. A drywall T-square works nicely for this.

STEP 4 Make and attach the leveling blocks. Install the T-nuts, locknuts, and leveling thumbscrews. Start a nylon-insert locknut onto the ends of the leveling screws, and adjust them all to the same height.

2

CUTTING STRAIGHT PROFILES

Key Ingredients

Shaping edges and adding molded profiles to a piece of furniture creates bands of light and shadow, bringing proportion, style, and grace to the piece. Imagine the cabinet shown in the photo with nothing but square edges. It would lose much of its visual appeal. Shaped edges are friendlier to the touch than sharp, square edges, and they also stand up to wear and tear better.

Shaping the edge of a piece of wood is one of the simplest ways to add a decorative element. Common examples include the edges of table tops, shelves, doors, and drawers. Wide profiles like crown molding and chair-rail molding are cut into the face of the stock rather than into the edge. Then the moldings are applied to furniture or to rooms. This difference is really just a matter of how the profile is oriented on the stock, and the shaping techniques themselves are generally identical whether you're cutting into the stock's edge or face. In every case the task is the same: safely producing the profile so the surface of the wood is smooth and consistent.

A practical way to distinguish among the techniques for cutting straight profiles has to do with how much of the face or edge you're

An assortment of profiled edges make this piece of frame-and-panel furniture interesting. (See the plans on page 97.) Although you must be concerned with the details of the shapes, the overall effect comes from the play of light and shadow on the profiles.

cutting away, as described below and shown in *Partial versus Full Shaping Cuts:*

Shaping part of an edge or face. This is the simplest situation because part of the edge remains intact and serves as a guide for making the cut.

Shaping all of an edge or face. When you make parts like a bullnosed molding or the edge of a stair tread, you have to shape the entire edge of the workpiece. Because the original jointed edge of the stock is being shaped away, it

can't serve to guide the cut—at least not in the same way.

Assorted applications of these two techniques are explored fully in the rest of this chapter and the book. (Note: Shaping curved edges, though similar in some respects to shaping straight edges, is treated separately in Chapter 3.)

Handheld versus Table Routing

With notable exceptions discussed throughout this book, the router is the tool most used for shaping edges. The bits available offer so many choices of shapes that the router is usually my first choice. Whenever you reach for a router bit, though, you face the questions: Should you take the workpiece to the router table? Or should you take the router to the workpiece? There's no single hard-and-fast rule, but here are some guidelines to keep in mind:

- Use the router table if the workpieces are small enough for you to manage comfortably. The router table is the best choice when you have a large number of parts, since freehand routing would require that you clamp and unclamp each piece.
- Use the handheld router on large pieces of wood that you can't easily lift by yourself or that would require cumbersome support on the router table.
- Use the router table for full edge cuts because these require a split fence.

FACT OR FICTION

SHAPING ON THE TABLE SAW?

People don't immediately think of the table saw as a shaping tool. But when a groove or rabbet is part of a more complex shape produced with another tool, you can usually save time by cutting the groove or rabbet on the table saw first. You can use a regular carbide blade or a dado set. The table saw is accurate and quick and has more than enough power for these cuts. It's also relatively safe, if you keep the cutter buried inside the wood. Always set up the table saw so the cut occurs as close to the fence as possible, instead of on the off side of the workpiece. You can use the miter gauge in conjunction with the rip fence to make crossgrain dadoes on the table saw. Since there's no waste piece to become trapped, there's no danger in using the rip fence as a stop while you push the workpiece and the miter gauge past the cutter.

- Use the router table when cutting with large or complex bits like panel raisers and cope-and-stick cutters. In most cases, the router table is the only practical way to use these bits. In all cases, the force these bits generate is so great that they're difficult to control in a handheld router.
- Making stopped cuts, like a stopped chamfer, is generally easier with a handheld router. Simply mark where you want to stop the cut, and stop when you get there. For large numbers of parts—a set of chair legs, for example—I'd take the trouble to set up stops on the router table fence. This ensures all the parts will be identical.

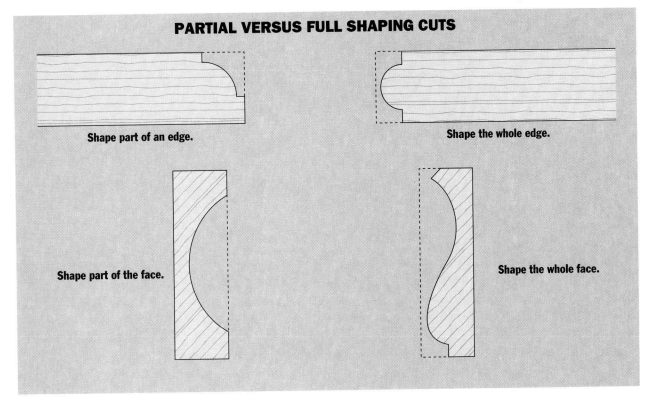

PARTIAL VERSUS FULL SHAPING CUTS

Shape part of an edge.

Shape the whole edge.

Shape part of the face.

Shape the whole face.

Shaping Part of a Straight Edge

Cutting a decorative profile into part of an edge is probably the most common router cut. There's no limit to the number and kind of router bits available for this task. But there are a limited number of good techniques for doing the job.

With a handheld router, you can guide the bit through the cut with a straight fence clamped to the workpiece. You can use a factory edge guide attached to the router, or you can make the one shown in "Pivoting Edge Guide." Or you can use a piloted bit that runs along the untouched portion of the edge itself. On the router table, you can guide the cut with a pilot or by running the stock against a straight fence. These examples are all shown in *Routing Part of a Straight Edge*. Other options for shaping part of a straight edge include the scratch stock (page 20), the hand plane (page 19), the table saw with a molding head (page 78), and the shaper (page 86).

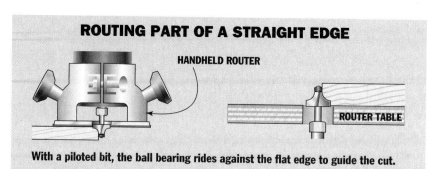

ROUTING PART OF A STRAIGHT EDGE

HANDHELD ROUTER

ROUTER TABLE

With a piloted bit, the ball bearing rides against the flat edge to guide the cut.

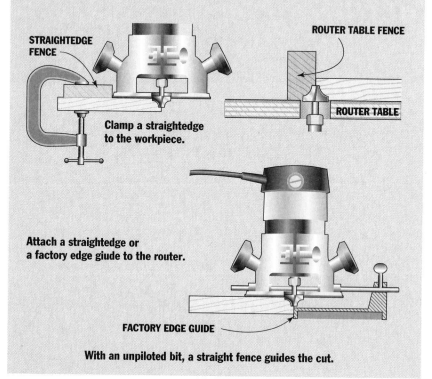

STRAIGHTEDGE FENCE

ROUTER TABLE FENCE

ROUTER TABLE

Clamp a straightedge to the workpiece.

Attach a straightedge or a factory edge giude to the router.

FACTORY EDGE GUIDE

With an unpiloted bit, a straight fence guides the cut.

SHOP SOLUTIONS: Pivoting Edge Guide

An adjustable edge guide, combined with the router's built-in depth adjustment, gives you precise control over the location of the cut. I use it for partial edge cuts, with router bits that don't have pilots, and for grooves and rabbets.

To make an adjustable guide, you need an oversized rectangular baseplate, as shown in the drawing. Drill several holes along one edge of the baseplate for anchoring one end of the edge guide. The spacing is not critical. Adjust the guide for the cut, and clamp the other end with a C-clamp. You can make a more sophisticated fence if you wish, but this simple one will get you started with your router.

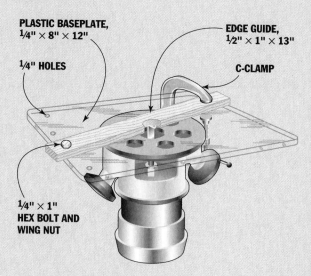

PLASTIC BASEPLATE, 1/4" × 8" × 12"

1/4" HOLES

EDGE GUIDE, 1/2" × 1" × 13"

C-CLAMP

1/4" × 1" HEX BOLT AND WING NUT

Problem Solving
Edge-Routing Troubles

Although edge routing is among the simplest router operations, there are a number of ways to end up with poor results. Here are a few problems to watch for and some ways to solve or avoid them.

PROBLEM	SOLUTION
The cut is ripply.	You are feeding the wood too quickly, causing it to vibrate against the cutter. Work at a slow, steady pace but don't stop altogether. Stopping in the middle of the cut can cause burn marks.
There are intermittent deep gouges in the routed surface.	In the case of the router table, you are not maintaining consistent contact between the wood and the fence. This is common when you are removing a lot of wood— the force of the bit kicks the wood away from the fence, especially when you shift your hand positions on the workpiece. Take a lighter cut, and add fingerboards to the setup.
There are intermittent burn marks on the routed profile.	Burn marks are caused when you hold the router still with the spinning bit against the wood. A dull bit makes burns more likely. Replace dull bits, and plan how to make the cut without stopping the router.
When you are working on the router table, the cut tapers toward one or both ends.	Either the fence or the edge of the wood is not straight. First check that the fence is straight. If it's not, replace it. Then check your workpiece by centering it against the fence. See if it rocks from end to end. See if you can slip the corner of a piece of paper or an automotive feeler gauge between the wood and the fence at any point. If you can do either, the wood is not straight and needs to be jointed.
The cut's rough, and the wood fibers are all torn and ragged.	You may be making too deep a cut or cutting against the grain. Take a shallower cut and make more passes, and if that doesn't clean it up, try a climb cut: moving the router opposite to the normal direction of feed. On the router table, don't try a climb cut without the help of feed wheels and work-holding fixtures like fingerboards.

Chamfering

Chamfering—cutting a simple 45-degree bevel—is a good example of shaping part of an edge. A chamfer tricks the eye into seeing a thick edge as a thinner edge. Take a 1-inch-thick table edge, for example, and cut a ½-inch chamfer into the underside of the edge, and the top will appear much lighter. Adding a ¼-inch chamfer to the top side of the edge makes the top look thinner still. Plus you create an interesting play of light on the chamfer's flat facet.

A chamfer is the easiest edge profile to make, and there are many ways to get the job done, as shown in *Four Ways to Chamfer.* The router and router table are the most convenient choices, followed by the jointer and table saw. Note that on the table saw and router table you want the edge you're chamfering to ride against the fence, so the workpiece is not trapped between the fence and the bit or blade. On the table saw, this means adding an auxiliary fence to bury the blade in.

Chamfering on the Router Table

When routing a chamfer on the router table, the setup depends upon the wood being straight and smooth and also on the router-table fence being straight and smooth. Adjust the width of a chamfer by moving the fence, not by raising or lowering the router itself. You can use a bit with a pilot or one without.

STEP 1 Install the bit in the collet, and raise most of the cutting edge above the table surface.

STEP 2 Unplug the router. Turn the cutter with your fingers so one flute is perpendicular to the fence. Then, bring the wood up to the cutter and adjust the fence by eye, making sure the point of the cutter and the steel pilot, if it has one, remain behind the front plane of the fence.

STEP 3 Slowly feed the first 6 inches of a piece of wood through the cutter. The workpiece should move easily and smoothly. Pull the workpiece straight away from the cutter, and inspect the cut. If it is not what you want, readjust the fence.

Chamfering with a Freehand Router

You don't need a router table to rout a clean chamfer or roundover. You can clamp the workpiece to the bench and rout the edge freehand. Here are some points to keep in mind:

● Half of the router base will rest on top of the workpiece and half will hang into space. To get the cleanest cut, apply downward pressure with one hand, while moving the router forward with the other.

● Whenever you rout freehand, clamp the workpiece to the top of the bench. Make sure the clamps won't interfere with the router's path, and that the electrical cord won't hang up on the clamps during the cut. Set the router on the edge of the workpiece to adjust the depth of cut.

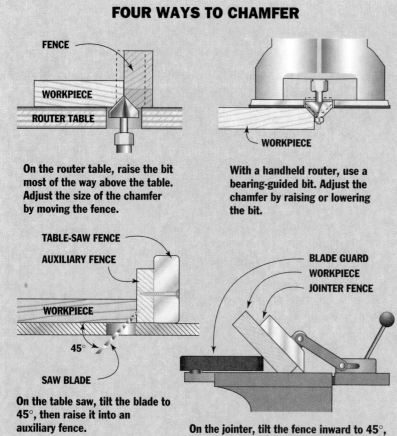

FOUR WAYS TO CHAMFER

FENCE
WORKPIECE
ROUTER TABLE

On the router table, raise the bit most of the way above the table. Adjust the size of the chamfer by moving the fence.

WORKPIECE

With a handheld router, use a bearing-guided bit. Adjust the chamfer by raising or lowering the bit.

TABLE-SAW FENCE
AUXILIARY FENCE
WORKPIECE
45°
SAW BLADE

On the table saw, tilt the blade to 45°, then raise it into an auxiliary fence.

BLADE GUARD
WORKPIECE
JOINTER FENCE

On the jointer, tilt the fence inward to 45°, then make full-length passes over the cutter until the chamfer is the desired width.

- When you are routing all the way around the workpiece, start the cut in the middle of one edge. Run the bearing hard into the wood. Go counterclockwise, so you can feel the resistance of the cutter against the wood. As you approach the corner of the workpiece, if you look through the openings in the router base, you'll be able to see when to turn.
- When you are only routing one edge, start near one end, rout forward, then cut backward to the other end of the workpiece. Chamfers and roundovers are safe cuts for learning how to feel the difference between routing in the normal direction and climb cutting.

CHAMFERING WITH A BLOCK PLANE

Chamfering with a hand plane is a quick and quiet alternative to the power tool techniques shown in *Four Ways to Chamfer*.

To plane a chamfer, you can stand the wood up on edge in the vise, or you can clamp it flat on the benchtop, extending out over the edge. Here are the steps to follow:

STEP 1 Pencil two light layout lines on the workpiece to mark the size of the chamfer, as shown in *Chamfering with a Block Plane*. After you've chamfered a few edges, you'll get confident holding the plane at a 45-degree angle, and you won't have to use layout lines.

STEP 2 Plane from one end of the workpiece to the other in one flowing motion. Swing your arm from the shoulder, not the wrist and elbow. At first you will remove only a tiny sliver of wood, but the shaving will get wider as you go deeper.

STEP 3 Set the plane fine for the last few strokes to finish the edge.

You'll find that you can take quite a deep cut to remove the bulk of the waste. If you set the iron of the block plane on an angle, so that one part of the edge will make a deep cut and one part will make a shallow cut, as shown in *Chamfering with a Block Plane*. You can hog off most of the waste and then make a finishing cut without stopping to adjust the plane.

To chamfer across the grain at the end of the board, hold the plane on an angle, as shown in *Chamfering End Grain*, and slice the wood away. The plane moves downward as it moves across the edge. The shearing cut prevents splintering.

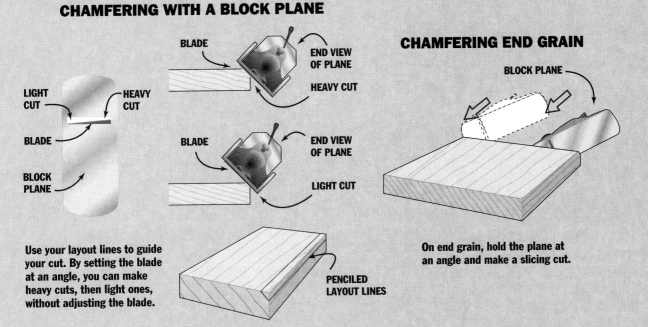

CHAMFERING WITH A BLOCK PLANE

BLADE

END VIEW OF PLANE

HEAVY CUT

LIGHT CUT — HEAVY CUT

BLADE

BLOCK PLANE

BLADE

END VIEW OF PLANE

LIGHT CUT

Use your layout lines to guide your cut. By setting the blade at an angle, you can make heavy cuts, then light ones, without adjusting the blade.

PENCILED LAYOUT LINES

CHAMFERING END GRAIN

BLOCK PLANE

On end grain, hold the plane at an angle and make a slicing cut.

Shaping Edges with a Scratch Stock

Routers are so good at shaping edges that many woodworkers look no further than a router bit catalog when trying to figure out how to mold a particular profile. That's too bad because some edge shapes are especially suitable to being cut with a simple hand tool known as a scratch beader, or more generally a scratch stock, as shown in the photo below.

The scratch stock is a simple tool that cuts a small profile into the corner of the wood. Once you've used it, you'll find that it often can get the job done more quickly than a router—and without any of the dust and noise. Shaping an edge with a shop-made scratch stock gives you the added pleasure of working with a tool you've made yourself.

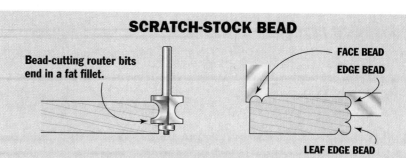

SCRATCH-STOCK BEAD

Bead-cutting router bits end in a fat fillet.

FACE BEAD
EDGE BEAD
LEAF EDGE BEAD

A scratch stock creates a more elegant bead and can be used with equal ease on edges and faces. Shaping a corner from both the face and the edge produces the leaf edge bead.

USING A SCRATCH STOCK ON CURVES

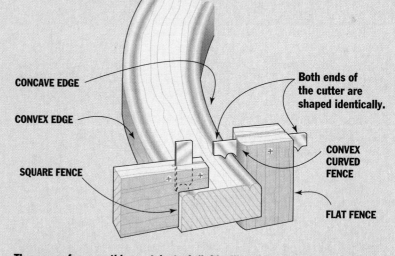

CONCAVE EDGE
CONVEX EDGE
SQUARE FENCE
Both ends of the cutter are shaped identically.
CONVEX CURVED FENCE
FLAT FENCE

The square fence on this scratch stock (left) will work on convex curved edges, but you need a tool with a curved fence to scratch concave edges. This scratch stock (right) has a curved edge on one side for beading concave edges and a flat edge on the other side for beading straight and convex edges.

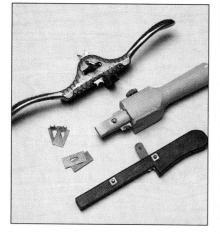

The scratch stock in the middle, made by Veritas, has cutters that fit the old Stanley (top) as well as my shop-made scratch stock (bottom). You can make cutters yourself from old hack-saw blades.

A scratch stock is a metal or wooden frame that holds a small, profiled cutter. The cutter is not ground with a sharp bevel, like a plane blade, nor is it held at an angle to the wood. It's more akin to a scraper blade, about the same thickness, and held roughly at 90 degrees to the surface of the wood. To use one, register the scratch stock fence against the edge or face of the workpiece. Hold it with both hands and keep it perpendicular to the edge. Scrape the wood with a series of light back-and-forth cuts, as shown in the photo on the opposite page. To start without skidding, press down lightly but firmly against the fence.

You can buy a scratch stock with a set of cutters, as shown in the photo at left, but it's easy to make this tool yourself, and then make cutters only as you need them. One of the most useful profiles to make with a scratch stock is the simple beaded edge, like the one shown in *Scratch-Stock Bead.* There are router bits that approximate this shape, as shown, but with a scratch stock, you can make the bead smaller and more delicate. It can

MAKING A SCRATCH STOCK

This scratch stock and cutter can be made and ready to use in a half hour. Follow these steps:

STEP 1 Saw a piece of hardwood to the dimensions in the drawing below, then make two saw cuts on the table saw to create the 90 degree inside corner. The short, vertical shoulder acts as the fence; the long arm holds the cutter.

STEP 2 Band-saw a kerf straight through the center of the arm and stop ½ inch *beyond* the shoulder. Extending the kerf gives you more flexibility when you want to use only part of a cutter.

STEP 3 Drill three holes for screws to hold the cutter in the arm.

STEP 4 Make the scratch stock cutter. Draw the shape you want on the edge of a scraper blade or a piece of hack saw blade. Trace the shape from an existing molding if possible. Grind the metal with a rotational stone held in a drill or Dremel tool. Use a file to fine-tune the shape, keeping the file perpendicular to the face of the cutter, then smooth both sides on a sharpening stone.

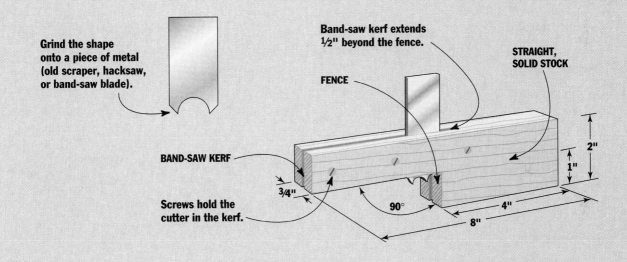

Grind the shape onto a piece of metal (old scraper, hacksaw, or band-saw blade).

Band-saw kerf extends ½" beyond the fence.

FENCE

STRAIGHT, SOLID STOCK

BAND-SAW KERF

Screws hold the cutter in the kerf.

¾" 90° 4" 8" 2" 1"

end in a nice sharp point, where a router bit has to end with a flat or listel. On straight stock, you can cut the bead into the edge, the face, or both, as shown.

You can also use a scratch stock to cut a bead onto a curved face or edge. On a convex curve, any scratch stock will work because the square face of the fence can follow the curve. For beading a concave curve, though, shape the face of the scratch stock convex so it can ride along the curve. See *Using a Scratch Stock on Curves.*

Work the scratch stock back and forth to scrape the profile into the wood.

Shaping the Whole Edge

When you shape the full edge of a board, there is no registration surface on the workpiece to guide the cut, so you need to find another way. You can clamp a straightedge to the workpiece to guide the router, as shown in *Routing All of a Straight Edge*, but I'd recommend that only for large workpieces that can't be taken to a router table. Otherwise, the process of clamping and unclamping is too slow. A better approach is to use a split fence on the router table—offsetting the outfeed side of the fence compensates for the depth of the cut, as shown.

The infeed side and the outfeed side of a split fence can be adjusted independently, like the infeed and outfeed tables on a jointer. You can shift the outfeed fence forward slightly to support the work as it leaves the cutter. *Split Fence for the Router Table* shows how to make a split fence. Slots routed in the regular router table fence permit each half of the split fence to be adjusted from side to side. Adjust each half of the fence so it will support the work right up to the cutting edges of the bit. (Plans for a router table and standard fence are on page 12.) "Using a Split Fence" below shows the basics of setting up a cut on a split fence, but here are some additional points to keep in mind:

● When adjusting the fence, you should aim to remove between $1/32$ and $1/16$ inch of the original

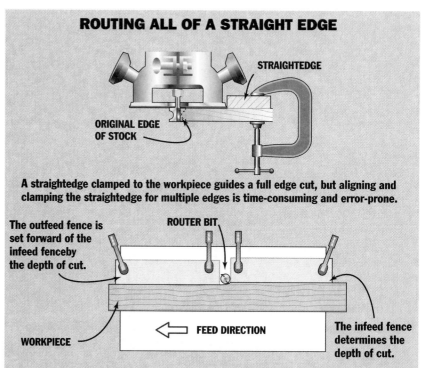

ROUTING ALL OF A STRAIGHT EDGE

STRAIGHTEDGE

ORIGINAL EDGE OF STOCK

A straightedge clamped to the workpiece guides a full edge cut, but aligning and clamping the straightedge for multiple edges is time-consuming and error-prone.

The outfeed fence is set forward of the infeed fence by the depth of cut.

ROUTER BIT

FEED DIRECTION

WORKPIECE

The infeed fence determines the depth of cut.

A split fence on the router table is a better technique.

STEP-BY-STEP: USING A SPLIT FENCE

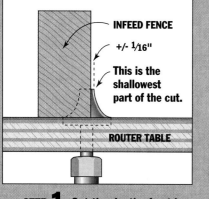

INFEED FENCE

+/- $1/16$"

This is the shallowest part of the cut.

ROUTER TABLE

STEP 1 Set the depth of cut by moving the infeed fence so it's about $1/16$ inch behind the cutting edge at the shallowest part of the cut.

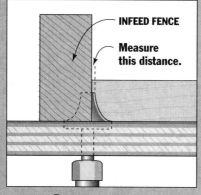

INFEED FENCE

Measure this distance.

STEP 2 Make a test cut part way along the edge of a board, and measure the depth of cut. Use a dial caliper if you have one.

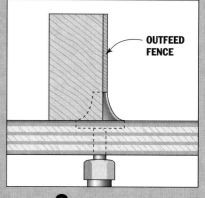

OUTFEED FENCE

STEP 3 Shim the outfeed fence forward from the infeed fence to the depth of cut you just measured.

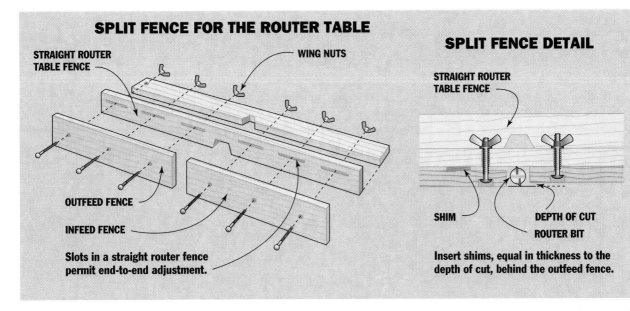

SPLIT FENCE FOR THE ROUTER TABLE

STRAIGHT ROUTER TABLE FENCE

WING NUTS

OUTFEED FENCE

INFEED FENCE

Slots in a straight router fence permit end-to-end adjustment.

SPLIT FENCE DETAIL

STRAIGHT ROUTER TABLE FENCE

SHIM

DEPTH OF CUT

ROUTER BIT

Insert shims, equal in thickness to the depth of cut, behind the outfeed fence.

edge of the stock. If you try to skim the edge of the stock, you may end up with an incomplete profile. Take more than $\frac{1}{16}$ inch and you're just wasting wood.

- Plastic laminate is pretty consistently $\frac{1}{16}$ inch thick, so it's worth saving scraps for fence shims. Playing cards work well, too. For ultra-precise adjustments, you can use simple Post-it notes. Each note is

$\frac{4}{1000}$ths of an inch thick so a stack of eight is $\frac{1}{32}$ inch.

- Both halves of a split fence must be parallel, and they must be dead straight. Otherwise, you won't get straight, consistent cuts.

Once both halves of the split fence are set, you make a full edge cut just like a partial edge cut. Move the workpiece at a steady rate past the cutter. If it's a large profile, make a series of lighter passes. But you'll need to decide on that before

setting up the split fence because the preliminary cuts will be partial edge cuts and should be done with the fence in its normal configuration. The sequence shown in "Using a Split Fence" is an example of this. It shows how to shape a bull-nosed edge using a round over bit. The first pass on all the stock is a standard cut because the uncut half of the edge rides against the fence. Only the second pass is a full edge cut requiring the split fence.

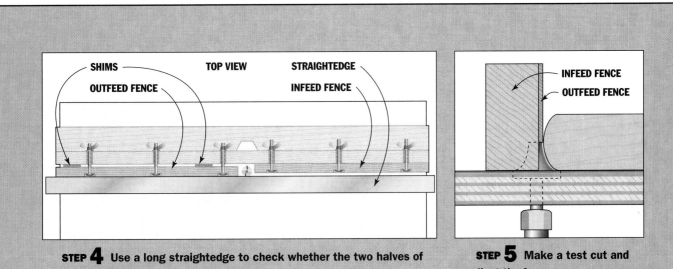

SHIMS   TOP VIEW   STRAIGHTEDGE

OUTFEED FENCE   INFEED FENCE

INFEED FENCE

OUTFEED FENCE

STEP 4 Use a long straightedge to check whether the two halves of the fence are parallel.

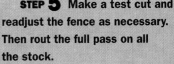

STEP 5 Make a test cut and readjust the fence as necessary. Then rout the full pass on all the stock.

Routing Cove Moldings

The cove, one of the basic shapes found in moldings, is basically a concave arc. It can be a symmetrical quarter circle, as shown in *Cove Molding*. This kind of molding completes the inside corner of a paneled room. Or it can be a broad, shallow section of a circle cut into the face of the stock to form crown molding, as also shown in the drawing.

On the router table, you can cut small cove moldings with a bearing-guided cove cutter or a core-box bit. Small moldings like

RIPPINGS

FITTING MOLDING TO UNEVEN WALLS

Walls and ceilings often have bumps and dips that make it difficult to fit a molding flush with the surfaces. What can you do? Cut a wide, shallow groove in the back of the molding. This "back relief cut" will bridge imperfections and give you an exact fit. If you intend to cut a back relief, do it before you mold the face.

BACK RELIEF CUT

Make the back relief cut before making other shaping cuts.

COVE MOLDING

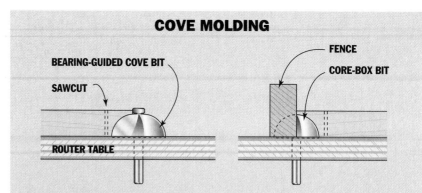

Cut small coves into the edge of wider stock, then rip the molding on table saw.

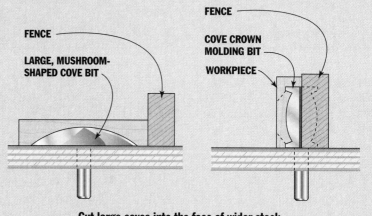

Cut large coves into the face of wider stock,
Then cut bevels on back to make crown molding.

This mushroom-shaped core-box bit is perfect for cutting medium-sized coves with the stock lying flat on the router table. Ripping a small groove in the wood helps locate the cove in the stock.

these should be shaped on the edge of wider stock, then ripped off the edge. You can rout modest-sized coves—up to 2 inches across the face—using a vertical router bit. With a wide mushroom-shaped core-box bit, run the stock flat on the router table, as shown in the photo. (See also the table-saw technique for cutting large cove molding on page 64.)

I prefer the bowl bit because it's safer to make the cut with the stock lying flat. It's easier to use the bowl bit for partial cove cuts on smaller moldings. With either bit, follow the sequence shown in "Routing a Deep Cove," keeping these points in mind:

● The bit should be centered in the width of the stock.
● The large cutter exerts a lot of pressure, so you should approach the final depth in stages of no more than $1/8$ inch.
● For the cleanest cut, feed the stock evenly and support it with fingerboards. You can produce a near-perfect surface straight from the router table.
● Complete the molding by routing or sawing a 45-degree bevel on all four corners, as shown in **STEP 3**.

RIPPINGS

AUXILIARY ROUTER TABLE SURFACE

Using large bits like a bowl bit or a horizontal panel raiser may mean you have to widen the hole in your router table or baseplate. But a large opening is unsafe when you go back to using a smaller bit because the workpiece is not supported close to the bit—where you need it most. Here's a better approach. Install the bit from above the table, and then fit an auxiliary table surface—a piece of $1/4$-inch-thick hardboard or Masonite—over the bit with a hole that's just big enough for the cutter. Clamp the hardboard to the router table, then clamp the fence in place as usual. You can also add an auxiliary table surface to make a small opening for very small cutters.

AUXILIARY ROUTER TABLE SURFACE

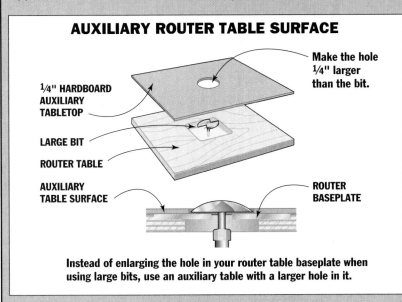

Make the hole $1/4$" larger than the bit.

$1/4$" HARDBOARD AUXILIARY TABLETOP

LARGE BIT

ROUTER TABLE

AUXILIARY TABLE SURFACE

ROUTER BASEPLATE

Instead of enlarging the hole in your router table baseplate when using large bits, use an auxiliary table with a larger hole in it.

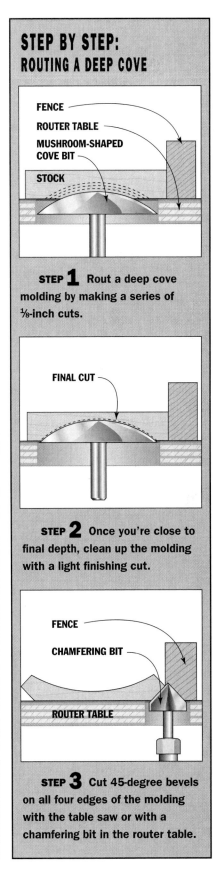

FENCE
ROUTER TABLE
MUSHROOM-SHAPED COVE BIT
STOCK

STEP 1 Rout a deep cove molding by making a series of $1/8$-inch cuts.

FINAL CUT

STEP 2 Once you're close to final depth, clean up the molding with a light finishing cut.

FENCE
CHAMFERING BIT
ROUTER TABLE

STEP 3 Cut 45-degree bevels on all four edges of the molding with the table saw or with a chamfering bit in the router table.

Using Vertical Molding Bits

Large molding profiles, such as chair rails and crowns, can be cut with a vertical router bit. These cutters are designed to take a full cut into the face of the stock and can be run against a split fence, as explained on page 22. But an easier approach is to rout the profile you want into the face of a board that is about ½ inch wider than the cutter. This leaves two ¼-inch bands of wood on the face intact to bear against the fence, as shown in *Using Vertical Molding Bits*. When you're done routing, you just saw the molding from the wide stock.

When using a vertical molding bit, follow these guidelines:

- Attach an auxiliary fence to the main router table fence. It should be tall enough to support the entire width of the stock.
- Work to the final shape in several light passes. Although these bits are designed to remove a lot of wood, trying to cut to final depth in one or two passes strains the router and can leave a wavy surface.
- Clamp a fingerboard to the router table so it presses the workpiece against the cutter. With the fingerboard in place right at the cutter, you can safely transfer hand pressure to guide the workpiece as it passes from one side of the cutter to the other.
- Feed the work slowly. A rippled cut shows you are feeding too fast.
- Because of the pressure from the fingerboard, vertical bits usually take a deeper bite,

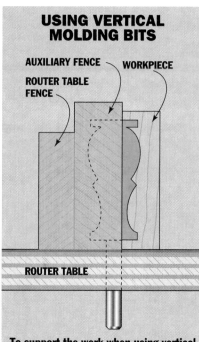

USING VERTICAL MOLDING BITS

AUXILIARY FENCE WORKPIECE
ROUTER TABLE FENCE

ROUTER TABLE

To support the work when using vertical bits, Rout profiles from stock that's wider than the bit profile. This leaves a portion of the face on the top and bottom edge to ride against the fence.

RIPPINGS

MAKING A CORNER BEAD WITH A ROUNDOVER BIT

You might think you can't make a corner bead with a piloted roundover bit because the bearing would get in the way. The solution is to make half of the cut first, as shown in the drawings. Then turn the stock to cut the other half. You may need to plane or sand the point where the two curves meet.

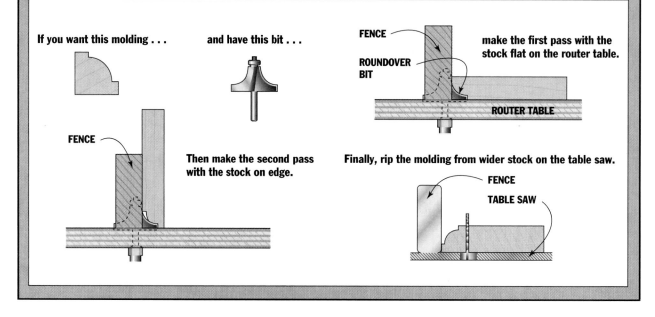

If you want this molding . . .

and have this bit . . .

FENCE

ROUNDOVER BIT

make the first pass with the stock flat on the router table.

ROUTER TABLE

FENCE

Then make the second pass with the stock on edge.

Finally, rip the molding from wider stock on the table saw.

FENCE

TABLE SAW

called snipe, just when the tail of the workpiece leaves the infeed fence. You can't really avoid snipe, so always make your wood a few inches longer than you need.

To cut a vertical molding like the one shown in the photo at right, follow this sequence:

STEP 1 Set the bit so that edges of the face of the stock ride against an auxiliary fence.

STEP 2 Install a fingerboard so it presses right at the cutter.

STEP 3 Rout the profile in several passes, feeding the stock slowly and steadily.

STEP 4 Saw or rout 45-degree bevels on the back edges of the molding.

A sturdy fingerboard keeps the stock tight against the fence when routing with a large vertical bit.

Problem Solving
Working with Narrow Pieces

Shaping narrow moldings can be difficult and dangerous. The thin workpiece can vibrate, ruining the cut. Or worse, the piece might break or split into pieces, kicking a shard of wood back at you.

PROBLEM	SOLUTION	
You want to make narrow moldings.	Shape the profile on the edges of wide boards. Routing the edges of wide boards is safer than trying to control narrow strips of wood. Also, the mass of the large piece dampens vibration, which makes for a cleaner cut. After shaping the edge, use the table saw or band saw to rip the moldings off the board. Then, run the edge of the board over the jointer, and repeat the sequence.	
You can't avoid routing a narrow strip.	When you shape and rip a series of narrow pieces from a wide board, the last piece is too small to work with but can still yield one last piece of molding. To shape such a narrow piece of stock safely, set up guide blocks and fingerboards on the router table. Then use the same kind of setup on the table saw to rip the molding to final width.	

Combining Shapes

A simple chamfer or roundover may be a suitable shape for the edge of a table with a simple design. Combining more than one shape to form a complex edge or molding can raise the quality of your woodworking designs. It's also sometimes necessary when your goal is to match a specific furniture style.

Even the most ornate molding is little more than a composition of small, simple shapes. To build these combinations, you need to work in one of two basic ways:

● You can mold a complex shape in a single piece of wood in stages, by combining a series of simple cutters, as shown in "Combining Simple Cutters." This works best when the shapes are simple and when the orientation of the separate shapes is such that you can cut them with standard router bits. But despite the optimistic diagrams in other router books, it's never easy to make complex shapes by combining multiple profiles, and sometimes it just isn't possible.

● Create the complex molding by making several simple moldings as separate pieces, then nail or glue them together, as shown in "Combining Simple Moldings." The complex moldings on traditional work usually are made of several simpler moldings. This approach generally uses less wood. It also allows you to make a mistake on one part of the molding and to recover without much loss.

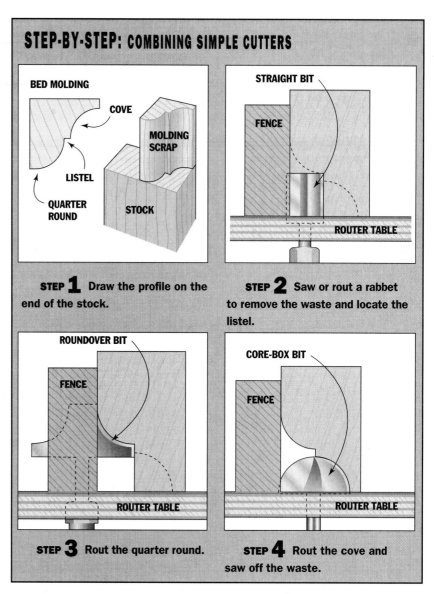

STEP-BY-STEP: COMBINING SIMPLE CUTTERS

STEP 1 Draw the profile on the end of the stock.

STEP 2 Saw or rout a rabbet to remove the waste and locate the listel.

STEP 3 Rout the quarter round.

STEP 4 Rout the cove and saw off the waste.

"Combining Simple Cutters" and "Combining Simple Moldings" show both approaches applied to making a bed molding, which combines a cove and a roundover separated by a flat land, or listel. Bed moldings are very common on traditional case furniture and also as a trim detail in period rooms. They are also used as standard crown moldings, as shown in the photo. This molding was cut with a single vertical cutter, as described in "Using Vertical Molding Bits" on page 26. No matter which approach

you take, here are some things to bear in mind:

● Expect to experiment. Until you have a lot of experience, you won't be able to plan your molding on paper and then go right to the perfect result. You have to draw the shape you want on the the wood, plan a series of cuts, and try it. You'll probably find that some portion of the sequence doesn't work the way you planned. You may find that some cuts just aren't possible with the bits you have, or that you need to change the sequence

The first sample (left) combines two simple moldings. The next one (middle) was routed with two simple edge cutters, plus a rabbeting bit. The third one (right) came off a single vertical cutter. All three moldings will look the same when installed on furniture or in a room.

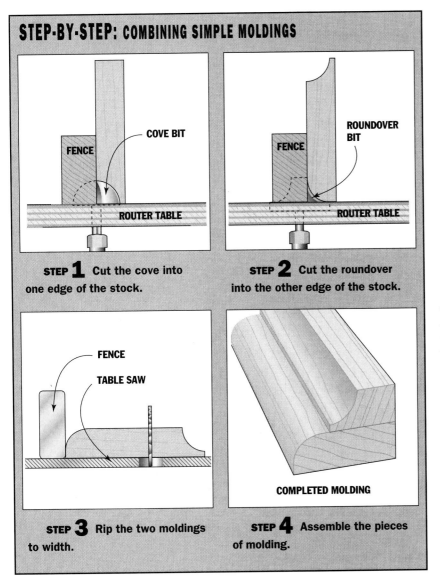

STEP-BY-STEP: COMBINING SIMPLE MOLDINGS

COVE BIT

FENCE

ROUTER TABLE

STEP 1 Cut the cove into one edge of the stock.

ROUNDOVER BIT

FENCE

ROUTER TABLE

STEP 2 Cut the roundover into the other edge of the stock.

FENCE

TABLE SAW

STEP 3 Rip the two moldings to width.

COMPLETED MOLDING

STEP 4 Assemble the pieces of molding.

to arrive at the final shape.

● Always avoid trapping the workpiece between the cutter and the fence because small pieces could easily be kicked back out of your hands. If you want to use just part of a profile, bury the rest of the cutter in the fence.

● Prepare extra stock to experiment with. You can't work out a complicated shape in scrap that's not the right size. You must work in the same material you intend to mold. I usually make an extra 6-foot length, which I cut into 18-inch test pieces. I usually don't need all four pieces, but you never know.

● Cutters with ball-bearing pilots usually cannot make portions of complex profiles. The pilot bearings get in the way. To make complex shapes, you need a set of simple cutters without pilots, as discussed in "Groove-Forming Bits" on page 8.

● Use the table saw to hog out most of the waste. When there is a land or a listel in the middle of a profile, establish it before you begin to rout by cutting a rabbet on the table saw.

When combining shapes, there are many hidden variables that affect the result you get, so something is certain to come out a little bit different than planned. If a piece of wood isn't quite straight or a little chip lodges against the fence, suddenly you've got a ridge where you expected one curve to blend smoothly into another. You can continue to fiddle with the setup, or you can plane and sand the trouble out of the finished piece. At some point you have to cut your losses and get on with your project. Nobody else will ever examine that molding as closely as you just did.

Applying Built-Up Crown Moldings

A classic form of crown molding used on tall cabinets is a large cove or ogee flanked by smaller complimentary moldings. Examples are shown in *Built-Up Crown Moldings*. I prefer to use the cove as the main element of a crown because you don't need a specialized bit to make it—you just use the large core-box bit, as shown on page 24, or the table-saw cove-cutting method that is found on page 64. On the other hand, the ogee style is readily available at home centers and lumberyards, and there's nothing wrong with store-bought molding if it's the size, shape, and species of wood you want.

You can experiment with the size of the components and their arrangemnt to find a pleasing combination for a project. You may be able to use the top of the cabinet itself as the top-most piece of molding. It's usually easier to add all the crown components as separate pieces, as shown in *Three-Part Crown Molding Detail*.

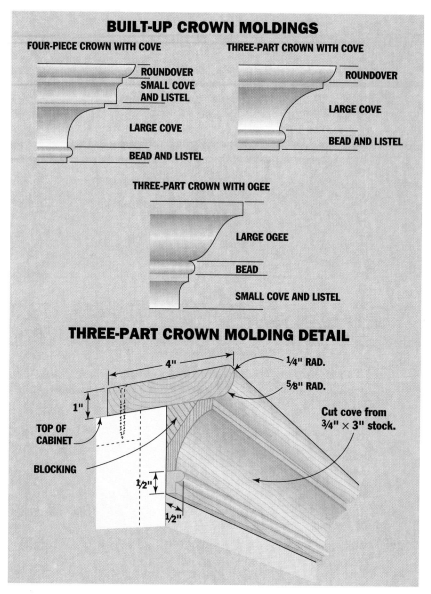

BUILT-UP CROWN MOLDINGS

FOUR-PIECE CROWN WITH COVE
- ROUNDOVER
- SMALL COVE AND LISTEL
- LARGE COVE
- BEAD AND LISTEL

THREE-PART CROWN WITH COVE
- ROUNDOVER
- LARGE COVE
- BEAD AND LISTEL

THREE-PART CROWN WITH OGEE
- LARGE OGEE
- BEAD
- SMALL COVE AND LISTEL

THREE-PART CROWN MOLDING DETAIL

- 4"
- 1"
- 1/4" RAD.
- 5/8" RAD.
- Cut cove from 3/4" × 3" stock.
- TOP OF CABINET
- BLOCKING
- 1/2"
- 1/2"

STEP-BY-STEP: SHAPING A BEAD AND LISTEL

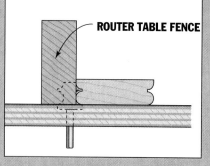

STEP 1 Rout the bead into both edges of a wide piece of stock.

ROUTER TABLE FENCE

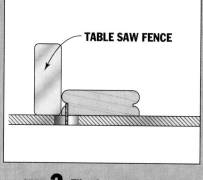

STEP 2 Flip the stock over and cut away the waste under the beads.

TABLE SAW FENCE

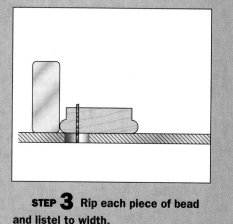

STEP 3 Rip each piece of bead and listel to width.

In general, the lower piece of molding serves as a seat for the crown so it gets tacked onto the structure itself. It could be a piece of square stock, but a bead and listel is also common. Cut the bead and listel from a single length of wood. Because it's a small piece of molding, start with wide enough stock so that you'll have something to hold while feeding it past the cutter on the router table. A smart approach is to get two pieces of molding from a single width, as shown in *Shaping a Bead and Listel*.

The cove requires a piece of blocking behind it for nailing or gluing and for supporting the molding above it. Once you've cut and sanded the cove molding, hold it against the cabinet to determine the shape of the blocking and the exact location of the bead and listel.

Cut all the loose moldings in as few pieces as possible. The fewer separate pieces you shape, the more consistent they'll be. Even small variations can be a pain when you miter moldings around a cabinet. For large moldings, like the crown cove, it's even worth cutting the pieces in sequence from the longer length. Then the grain continues smoothly around the cabinet. Sand the molding before installing it, then just blend the miters afterward. Once you've got all the moldings and blocking ready, apply them from the bottom up, and from the front to the sides.

SHOP SOLUTIONS: Router Table Stock Supports

To rout long lengths of cove or any other molding, you need to devise a way to support the stock on both the infeed side and the outfeed side. The drawing shows a pair of simple plywood stock supports clamped to the router table fence. You still need to hold the stock securely right at the cutter, either with your hands or with fingerboards. But the supports make starting and finishing the cut on long stock much easier.

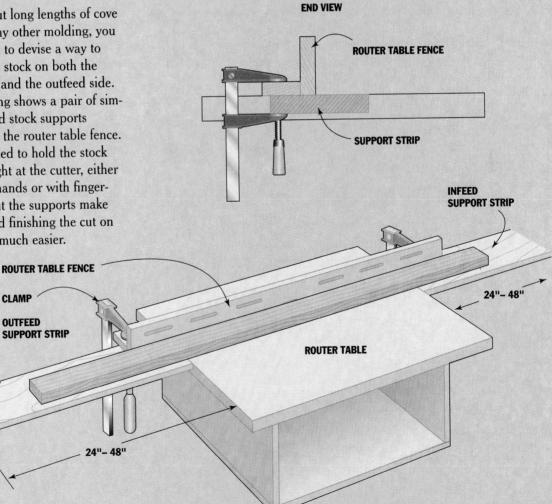

END VIEW

ROUTER TABLE FENCE

SUPPORT STRIP

INFEED SUPPORT STRIP

24"– 48"

ROUTER TABLE FENCE

CLAMP

OUTFEED SUPPORT STRIP

ROUTER TABLE

6"

24"– 48"

Smoothing Shapes and Profiles

When it comes time to prepare the surface of shapes and profiles for finish, you really only have two choices: You can sand it, or you can scrape it. Sanding shapes and profiles is tedious because you can't take advantage of power sanders to speed the job along. You have to hand-sand every nook and cranny with a couple grits of paper. Note that sandpaper tends to crush the wood fibers, so to get good results, you have to sand all the wood consistently.

Scraping works differently. With a sharp scraper, you can smooth a surface in a couple quick passes. But the scraper has to fit the molding precisely or it will leave bands of unscraped wood. If you can make a scraper to fit a molding perfectly, scraping is the way to go. Otherwise, you'll have to sand.

Sanding the Shapes

The trick to sanding shaped wood is getting the sandpaper to conform to the shape. Simple convex shapes like roundovers and bullnoses can be hand sanded easily because your hand itself molds to the shape. With more intricate moldings, the sandpaper doesn't quite reach into the corners or coves, so it mashes those convex elements you want to remain crisp.

The friction from sanding also can burn your fingers.

A better approach is to make a shaped block that's the inverse, or counterprofile, of the molding. Before you start, check to see if the molding itself might already provide its own inverse, like the bed molding does in the photo below left.

There are three good approaches for making shaped sanding blocks. Each requires creating the counterprofile of the molding and then using it as the sanding block.

For large simple shapes, like a cove, you can band-saw the coun-

Sometimes you get lucky, and a molding makes its own sanding block, like this bed molding.

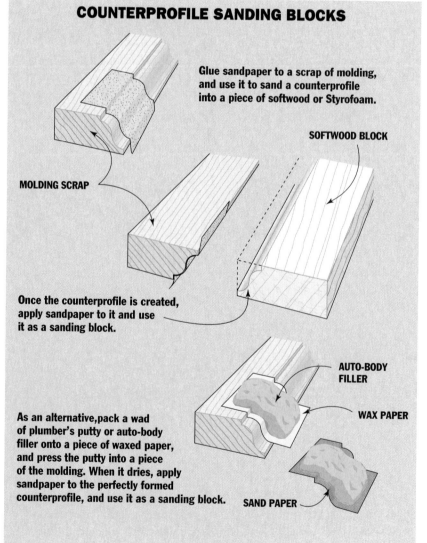

COUNTERPROFILE SANDING BLOCKS

Glue sandpaper to a scrap of molding, and use it to sand a counterprofile into a piece of softwood or Styrofoam.

SOFTWOOD BLOCK

MOLDING SCRAP

Once the counterprofile is created, apply sandpaper to it and use it as a sanding block.

AUTO-BODY FILLER

WAX PAPER

As an alternative, pack a wad of plumber's putty or auto-body filler onto a piece of waxed paper, and press the putty into a piece of the molding. When it dries, apply sandpaper to the perfectly formed counterprofile, and use it as a sanding block.

SAND PAPER

terprofile onto a block of wood, then sand the block to fit the molding. Apply sticky-backed sandpaper to the counterprofile, and you have a long-lasting sanding block for that shape.

For moderately complex moldings that can't be band-sawn, use the molding itself to create the counterprofile. Glue a layer of coarse grit sandpaper to a scrap of the molding, as shown in *Counterprofile Sanding Blocks*. Sticky-backed sandpaper makes the job easy. Use this to sand the counterprofile into a block of soft pine or basswood, or try a piece of dense styrofoam—the kind used as insulation board. Then glue a medium- or fine-grit sandpaper into the softwood block to complete your fitted sanding block.

The third approach is a little messy but it gives the best results when sanding an intricate profile. Press a mound of plumber's putty

or auto-body filler and a layer of wax paper onto a section of the molding. When the putty dries, lift it off, apply sandpaper, and you've got the most precise counterprofile sanding block you can make.

Scraping the Shapes

Like a French curve, a gooseneck scraper can work its way into many concave profiles. But if you are working a more complex molding profile, your best bet is to shape an ordinary steel scraper to fit exactly, as shown in "Making a Shaped Scraper." Shape to the line with a grinder or Dremel tool, and clean up the cut with files. The technique is the same as you'd use to make scratch stock cutters, as described in "Making a Scratch Stock" on page 20. To scrape a molding, hold the scraper nearly perpendicular to the wood and move it back and forth.

A gooseneck scraper easily smooths the torn fibers inside this large cove molding. Coves cut on the table saw may have deep saw marks, and scraping is a shortcut to the final surface.

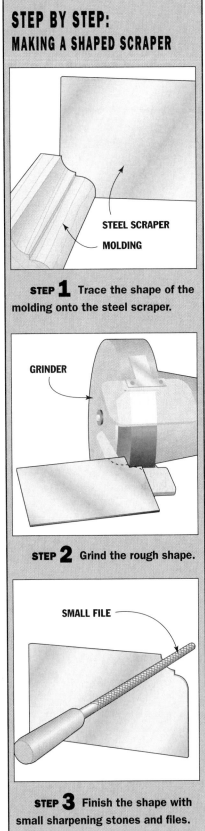

STEP BY STEP: MAKING A SHAPED SCRAPER

STEEL SCRAPER
MOLDING

STEP 1 Trace the shape of the molding onto the steel scraper.

GRINDER

STEP 2 Grind the rough shape.

SMALL FILE

STEP 3 Finish the shape with small sharpening stones and files.

3
CUTTING AND SHAPING CURVES

Key Ingredients

Curves add spice and vitality to a design, but they also add complication. Since most woodworking machinery operates in a straight line, when you cut or mold a straight edge, an ordinary straight fence is all the guide you need. But a straight fence can't help you saw or mold a curved edge.

This isn't that big a deal when you just need a single curve. You can cut it freehand on a band saw, and sand or scrape it to shape. But when you need two or more identical curves, it's far easier to make a template or pattern of the curve you want, and then to devise a method for tracing that pattern with a saw blade, router bit, or even an abrasive.

To make a pattern, you still have to lay out and shape the curve by hand once. After that, you can make as many duplicates as you want. Shape the first part by hand from an easy-to-work wood like pine or poplar. Then use the original part to make a durable master pattern from a sheet material like hardboard, medium-density fiberboard, or plywood. Make all subsequent parts from the master pattern. (Or you can simply use your original for

When building projects with curved parts, it pays to take the time to make accurate templates to reproduce the curves. The rails for this folding screen were pattern-sawn and -routed using half patterns, as described on pages 38–43.

a pattern, but it probably won't be as durable.) For complete details on making patterns, see "Cutting Curves" on page 36.

One thing to keep in mind: Cut all the joinery in the curved pieces first, before shaping them. You need straight, square edges from which to measure and to use as guides for your tools.

Pattern sawing, pattern routing, and pattern sanding can work hand in hand to produce any manner of

curved shapes. As a general strategy, it's always better to remove waste wood as a solid lump—by sawing it—instead of as a cloud of chips and dust. While it may be possible to rout a curved part directly from a square blank, it's hard on the router, and by the time you breathe the dust and sweep the chips, it's hard on you, too. So the sequence is as follows: Saw most of the waste off, then rout to the final shape, and sand smooth.

Pattern Followers

To get a machine to trace a pattern, you must arrange a follower in relation to the cutter. The follower guides the cut much as a fence does with a straight cut. For pattern sawing, the follower is usually shop-made, often no more that a strip of wood clamped to the band-saw table. For pattern routing, you have a few more choices.

Some straight router bits come with an attached bearing (usually the same diameter as the cutting diameter of the bit) that can ride along a pattern. (See *Straight Bits* on page 8.) These bits are available with the bearing either at the end (known as flush-trim bits), or between the flutes and the shank (called pattern-cutting bits). Flush-trim bits work well with a table-mounted router because the pattern can be mounted on top of the workpiece, where you can see it. Pattern-cutting bits work best with handheld routers because the pattern can be mounted on top of the workpiece. They are also handy when you don't want to have to rout all the way through a workpiece. Both types of bits reproduce the pattern exactly.

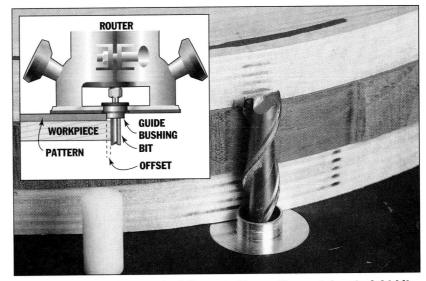

Guide bushings allow you to follow a pattern with a regular straight bit. The line of cut is offset from the edge of the template.

Guide bushings, or guide collars, mount to the base of a router and surround the bit, as shown in the photo above. For clearance, guide bushings must have a larger inside diameter than the bit itself. However, this means they will reproduce the pattern at a slightly larger or smaller size in the workpiece. The size difference between the cutter and the guide bushing is called the offset distance. It's handy to have a range of guide bushings so you can choose the offset that is most convenient. For more details,

see "Making Offset Patterns" on page 41.

Wood shapers, as discussed more fully on page 86, are excellent machines for pattern work. One style of pattern follower is a steel ring mounted on the spindle above the cutter. The ring, (or rub collar), can be the same size as the cutter diameter, or it can be offset.

Rub collars are also available in the form of large ball bearings. The scale of a shaper is larger than a router setup, but the idea is exactly the same. Some woodworkers prefer to use a guide bushing attached to the shaper fence above the cutter. It's called a ring fence.

Molding Curves

Once you've created a curved edge, molding it is easy. If you only want to shape part of the edge, the workpiece can serve as its own pattern, as shown in *Molding Part of a Curved Edge*. To shape the entire edge, guide the bit along the template you made to create the curve in the first place, as shown in *Molding All of a Curved Edge*.

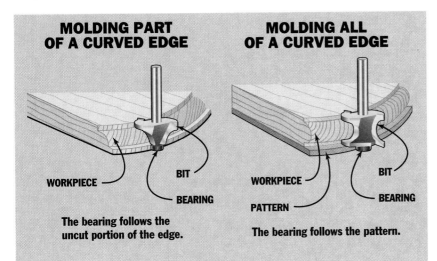

MOLDING PART OF A CURVED EDGE

WORKPIECE — BIT — BEARING

The bearing follows the uncut portion of the edge.

MOLDING ALL OF A CURVED EDGE

WORKPIECE — BIT — BEARING
PATTERN —

The bearing follows the pattern.

Cutting Curves

When you want to make a curved shape, you have to lay it out, saw it, and clean up the edges, as shown in "Making Curved Shapes." Once you've made one, you can use the original as a pattern to saw additional copies. However, if I have to make more than one or two copies, I use the original piece to make a more durable pattern from plywood or medium density fiberboard (MDF). Often these patterns will have built-in clamps and other holddowns to make shaping the pieces easier.

Draw a full-sized layout on paper, and work out all the curves on the drawing. Don't leave unsolved problems to transfer onto the wood. Where one curve meets another, use french curves to blend the lines together. Flexible splines and compasses are also useful for drawing fair curves.

When you're satisfied with the drawing, glue it directly onto your workpiece with spray adhesive or rubber cement.

Band-Sawing to a Line

The band saw is the tool of choice for sawing curved shapes. For general work, use a 1/4-inch, 6 tooth-per-inch blade. Start by making straight relief cuts from the edge of the blank into the deepest corners and curves, as shown in "Making Curved Shapes." Go straight in, cutting almost to the line, then back straight out. Relief cuts release the waste as you cut past them, giving the saw blade room to manuever.

Feed the work into the band-saw blade and keep your eye on where the blade is cutting. Turn corners by swinging the workpiece while you feed it into the blade. Concentrate on keeping the blade tangent to the curve you want to saw. If you try to make the cut turn without also

advancing the workpiece, the blade will bind and may break.

Saber-Sawing to a Line

A handheld saber saw works the same way as the band saw: The blade always cuts a tangent to a curve, and it must go forward in order to turn. Because the saw has no bottom guide, you need a sensitive touch and some practice to steer it forward as you steer along the cutting line. If you press sideways, the blade may continue to follow the line on top of the work, but it will bend sideways inside the wood and create a beveled edge. While a band saw is the better tool for most jobs, a saber saw is my choice for cutting curves in large, unwieldy pieces. It also can make interior cutouts that the band saw can't.

Smoothing a Curved Edge

Clean up a curved saw cut by planing and sanding to the line.

STEP-BY-STEP: MAKING CURVED SHAPES

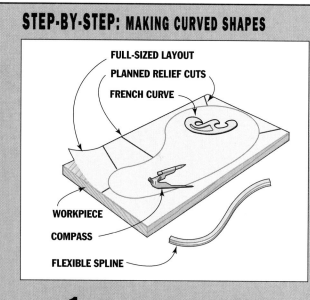

FULL-SIZED LAYOUT
PLANNED RELIEF CUTS
FRENCH CURVE
WORKPIECE
COMPASS
FLEXIBLE SPLINE

STEP 1 Lay out your curve full size on paper, using a compass, french curve, or flexible spline. Plan relief cuts as you lay out. Then glue the layout to your workpiece.

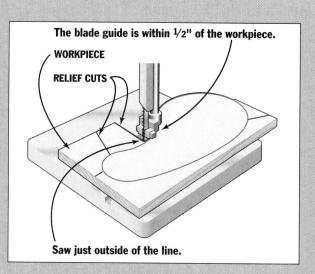

The blade guide is within 1/2" of the workpiece.
WORKPIECE
RELIEF CUTS
Saw just outside of the line.

STEP 2 Make the relief cuts, then saw the shape, staying just outside the layout line. Feed the stock through the blade with a fluid motion to achieve the smoothest curves.

Work the concave parts of the curve first, using a round-bottomed spokeshave. Pull the tool toward you, and always work downhill, with the grain. Smooth the convex portions of the curve with a flat spokeshave or a block plane. Pay attention to grain direction, and hold the tool at a slight skew angle to the edge of the wood so it slices the fibers. A Surform or a patternmaker's rasp can help you in areas where the grain changes direction, such as at the bottom of a valley.

Make a curved sanding block (or blocks) to do the final finishing. You may have to sand torn grain, and you'll have to blend, or fair, the curves into one another where they change direction. Ideally, the curve of the block should match the curve you're after. Sight the edges and run your hand over them to see if the curves are fair, that is, without lumps and divots. You'll be able to see and feel when you have it right.

Problem Solving
Forming a Curve

Forming fair, true curves requires patience and sensitivity. Unfortunately, curves that aren't true look pretty bad.

PROBLEM	SOLUTION
I'm having trouble working the entire edge of a tabletop to the layout line with my spokeshave.	Try beveling one corner down to the line first. Then gradually extend the bevel across the full edge. By working one corner first, you're removing less wood so the tool is easier to control.
I have trouble sawing to a line. My band saw seems to wander about as if it has a mind of its own.	First, check to make sure that the blade is properly tensioned and that the guide blocks are in close so the blade can't wiggle around. Then as you're cutting, try to make the cut in one or two graceful motions rather than by steering the board inch by inch.

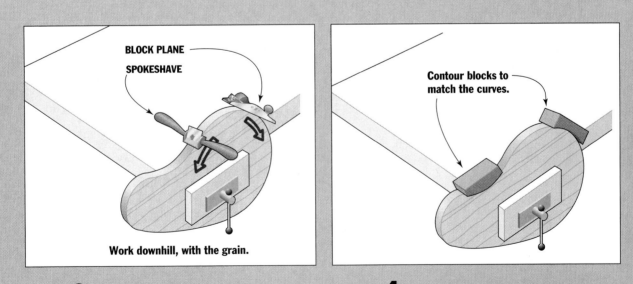

BLOCK PLANE
SPOKESHAVE

Work downhill, with the grain.

Contour blocks to match the curves.

STEP 3 Smooth and true the curves with a plane, a spokeshave, or a stationary disk or drum sander.

STEP 4 Make a curved block or blocks to do the final smoothing. Sand the curves fair to one another.

Pattern Sawing

Pattern sawing on the band saw is a good way to duplicate simple curved parts. The technique works especially well in combination with template routing and pattern sanding. First you pattern-saw to remove most of the waste, then you pattern-rout and/or sand to refine the shape.

To pattern-saw, attach the template or the original part to a blank. Then clamp a wooden follower to the band-saw table, as shown in the photo below. The band-saw blade rides in a notch in the follower, which rubs against the pattern. When you guide the pattern against the follower, the band saw cuts a duplicate shape in the wooden blank.

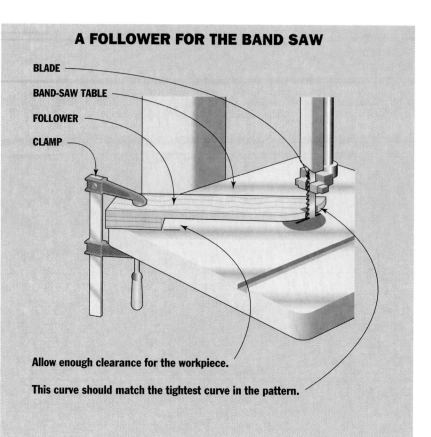

A FOLLOWER FOR THE BAND SAW

BLADE

BAND-SAW TABLE

FOLLOWER

CLAMP

Allow enough clearance for the workpiece.

This curve should match the tightest curve in the pattern.

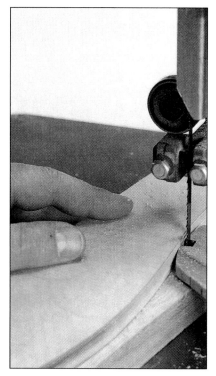

Pattern sawing on the band saw is a fast way of cutting parts to shape. With a sharp blade and a well-tuned saw, the part should require very little cleanup.

Make the follower, as shown in *A Follower for the Band Saw*, to dimensions that fit your saw. You can make it for either side of the blade, but there's more clearance for larger pieces if you attach it on the column side.

The follower can trace a pattern attached to the top of the workpiece or to its underside. I prefer the pattern on top of the workpiece because it is easier to see what's going on. Add shims under the clamped end to adjust the height of the follower above the table so the workpiece can fit underneath.

The curve in the follower has to be just smaller than the tightest curve in the pattern. If it's too small, steering the stock smoothly becomes difficult. If the curve is too flat, the blade won't reach the deepest hollows, and you won't be able to saw out your space accurately.

Attach the pattern to the workpiece with double-sided carpet tape. Its grip is strong enough to permit you to cut without any other means of attachment. For an even stronger bond, squeeze the pattern/tape/workpiece sandwich with clamps or in a vise before cutting. If you squeeze things too much, however, you may not be able to get the pieces apart.

RIPPINGS

CLONING REPAIR PARTS

When repairing furniture, you can pattern-saw a replacement part by using the original as a template. Even when the original part has been badly damaged, usually you can stick it together well enough to saw a copy. If part of the original is missing, try patching it with plumber's putty or auto-body putty.

PATTERN SAWING ON THE TABLE SAW

While you can't use a table saw for curved parts, it can reproduce any straight-sided part that doesn't have concave cutouts. The drawing shows the basic setup.

Because you're sawing a series of straight lines, the contact between follower and pattern should also be a straight line. Otherwise, the logic is the same as when reproducing a curved part on the band saw. If you're only making a few parts, attach the pattern to the blank with double-sided carpet tape. If you're making many parts, drive small screws or brads through the pattern so their points grab the workpiece.

Screw the follower and its bracket to the spacer, and attach the jig to the rip fence. Adjust the fence so the edge of the follower is flush with the outside of the blade.

Make sure the spacer is thicker than the workpiece so there's clearance, and make sure there's enough room for the waste to clear between the blade and the spacer. Saw the workpiece by guiding each edge of the pattern along the follower.

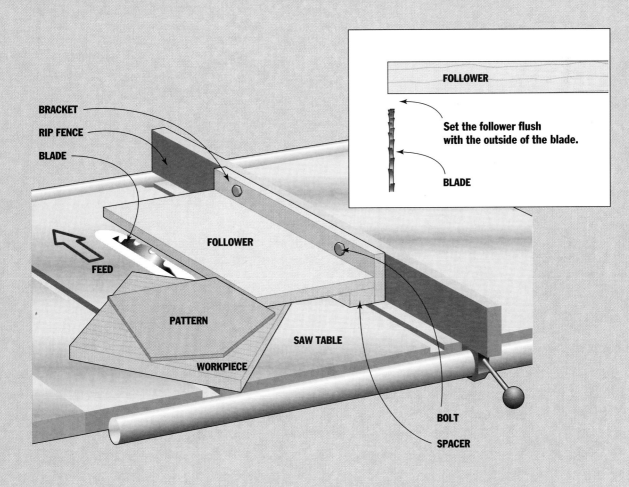

BRACKET

RIP FENCE

BLADE

FEED

FOLLOWER

PATTERN

WORKPIECE

SAW TABLE

BOLT

SPACER

FOLLOWER

Set the follower flush with the outside of the blade.

BLADE

If you plan to pattern-rout or pattern-sand the parts after sawing them, set up the follower so the blade is inset into the opening about $\frac{1}{16}$ inch or so. This leaves the workpieces a little larger than the pattern.

Leaving a little stock for cleanup means you can use the same pattern with your table-mounted router or stationary sander to trim the stock to final size. For more details, see "Pattern Routing" on page 40 and "Pattern Sanding" on page 42.

Pattern sawing is a powerful technique for making multiples. With a well-tuned band saw, often only a light sanding is necessary before the pieces are ready for finish.

Pattern Routing

In principle, pattern routing is no different from pattern sawing: Attach a template to the work-piece, and trace it with a follower, such as a bit-mounted ball bearing. In practice, the grain of the wood introduces a problem you don't have when sawing. In order to avoid tear-out, you must always rout downhill, with the grain.

With curved work, this is a key consideration because if you rout the full length of a curve, somewhere you'll be cutting uphill, as shown in *Grain Direction*. Routing against the grain almost guarantees torn grain. The solution is to change direction part way along the curve, so you're always cutting downhill, with the grain. Since you can't change the way a router bit spins, this means turning the workpiece over and working from the other side.

There are two categories of pattern-routing jigs: half-pattern jigs

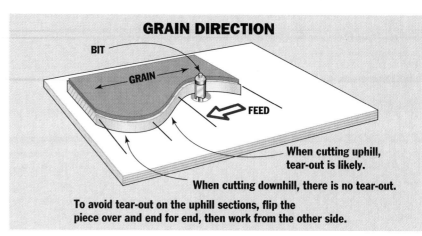

GRAIN DIRECTION

BIT

GRAIN

FEED

When cutting uphill, tear-out is likely.

When cutting downhill, there is no tear-out.

To avoid tear-out on the uphill sections, flip the piece over and end for end, then work from the other side.

and sandwich jigs. I prefer the simpler half-pattern whenever it can do the job. Both kinds of jig are generally used on the router table. For large work, you could clamp a pattern to the piece and trace it with a handheld router.

Half-Pattern Jigs

When you want to rout a symmetrical part, use a half-pattern jig, like the one shown in the photo at left. Since you can't rout the whole shape at once, you don't need to make a pattern for the whole shape. Make and use a half-pattern like this:

STEP 1 Lay out half the curve on paper. Glue the paper to a piece of easy-to-work wood like pine.

STEP 2 Cut out the curve, then sand and trim it to shape.

STEP 3 Attach the wooden pattern to a piece of plywood or MDF that is large enough to serve as a carrier for the entire workpiece. Cut the plywood roughly to shape, then rout it true to the wooden pattern with a flush-trim bit. Add fences and stop blocks to locate the workpiece on the pattern, as shown in *Half-Pattern Jig*.

STEP 4 Rough out the workpiece on the band saw. You can use the same jig to pattern-saw the piece, or you can saw it freehand.

STEP 5 Fit the workpiece into the jig and rout to or from the center line, according to the grain direction. Flip the workpiece over and/or end to end to shape its other half.

Sandwich Jigs

A sandwich jig traps the workpiece between two identical pat-

A half-pattern jig holds the workpiece while you rout half of the shape. Release the clamps, turn the workpiece over and end for end, and cut the second part of the curve.

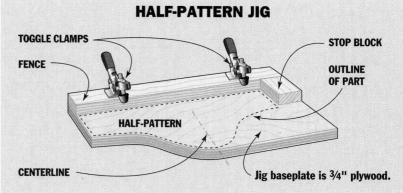

HALF-PATTERN JIG

TOGGLE CLAMPS

FENCE

HALF-PATTERN

CENTERLINE

STOP BLOCK

OUTLINE OF PART

Jig baseplate is ¾" plywood.

terns, as shown in *Sandwich Jig*. You avoid tear-out by flipping the whole assembly over whenever the grain changes direction. Marks on the jig locate the change points. Bolts and T-nuts act as clamps.

To turn the jig over, you must start and stop the router cut, and there's always a risk that the router will grab the work. The solution is to equip your router table with a starting pin, as shown in the photo at right. The pin acts as a fulcrum, helping you ease the workpiece into the cutter. When you feel the pattern contact the bearing, pivot it off the starting pin and begin the cut.

Sandwich jigs are complex to make but worth the trouble when you want to shape a lot of identical parts. Here's how to make one:

STEP 1 Make up two identical patterns. Take a workpiece blank that has been accurately cut to size, and trace its outline on one of the patterns. Locate the bolt positions

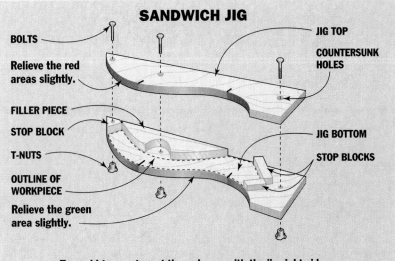

SANDWICH JIG

BOLTS
Relieve the red areas slightly.
FILLER PIECE
STOP BLOCK
T-NUTS
OUTLINE OF WORKPIECE
Relieve the green area slightly.
JIG TOP
COUNTERSUNK HOLES
JIG BOTTOM
STOP BLOCKS

To avoid tear-out, rout the red area with the jig right side up.
Rout the green area with the jig upside down.

on this pattern, avoiding the area where the workpiece will be. Two or three bolts are usually enough.

STEP 2 Clamp the patterns together. Drill and counterbore the bolt holes.

STEP 3 Locate stop blocks on one of the two patterns to position

the workpieces. Try to locate the stop blocks so the pieces only can fit into the jig one way. The stop blocks should be slightly thinner than the workpiece so the workpiece is held securely when the bolts are tightened.

STEP 4 Add filler pieces in between the patterns if tightening the bolts distorts the patterns. The fillers should be the same thickness as the workpiece. They don't have to fit tightly against the workpiece, but they can if you want to use them as part of the stop block system.

STEP 5 Clamp the workpieces between the patterns and rout them to shape.

No matter how accurately you make the sandwich jig, there's usually enough play in the bolts to prevent the curves from fairing smoothly into one another. You can achieve some adjustment by sanding away (or relieving) the pattern where it's not being followed, as shown. Finally, however, you may have to sand the transitions where the cuts stop and start.

RIPPINGS

MAKING OFFSET PATTERNS

If you're pattern-routing using guide bushings, the pattern has to be smaller than the workpiece. The amount is equal to the offset between the bushing and the bit (bushing radius – bit radius = offset). To make an offset pattern, make a master template to the exact size you want the finished workpiece to be. Fasten a pattern blank to the master and cut it to shape by tracing the master with a rabbeting bit in a router. The rabbeting bit will leave the pattern smaller than the master. By using the appropriate bearing on the bit, you can make the size difference equal to the offset you're after.

A sandwich jig permits you to rout downhill by flipping the assembly when the wood grain changes direction. The white plastic peg is a starting pin, which helps in starting and stopping the cut.

Pattern Sanding

As an alternative to routing, you can pattern-sand a sawn part to clean it up. Use a drum sander on the drill press. You can get a sanding drum with a phenolic follower on the bottom, as shown in the photo. It works like a flush-trim router bit. You can make your own follower by screwing a wooden disk the same diameter as the drum to the table under the drum. With either setup, attach the pattern to the underside of the workpiece.

You can pattern-sand with almost any type of pattern. The two-sided jig shown in the photo above is a way of speeding up the work. It holds two workpieces at one time, shaping the concave side of one of them and the convex side

Once you're familiar with using patterns, there is no end to how you can make them. This two-sided jig holds two workpieces, so you can sand the outside edge of one and the inside edge of the other. at the same time.

of the other. Then you swap the workpieces to complete the operation.

The two-sided jig can also be used on the router table. However, when you rout, part of the cut will be uphill, against the grain. You can avoid tear-out by climb cutting (cutting with the rotation of the cutter) part of the curve. Climb cutting is safe if you are only removing a small amount of wood at one time, which this jig is designed to do.

A Pattern-Cutting Demonstration

The techniques of pattern sawing and pattern sanding can be combined to shape any number of curved pieces, such as the crest rail of a chair back. This demonstration will show you how to move back and forth from one machine to the other to create a finished curved part.

Begin by cutting the workpiece blanks to finished length and width, as shown in "Pattern Cutting a Crest Rail." If they're going to be tenoned, do it now, while the wood is square. Bandsaw and sand a full-sized, one-sided pattern of the rail's curve. Note that while the pattern is concave, the first cut is for the convex side of the rail. The back of the pattern should be flat so you can attach it to the blank.

Attach the pattern to the workpiece with double-sided carpet tape. Also tape a support block—a rectangular scrap about 3 inches square, with the corners knocked off—to the band-saw fence to serve as a follower. Saw the work-

piece by running the curved face of the pattern against the support block. This cut doesn't make the full curve, it just removes the thick part of the waste.

Now take the workpiece to the disk sander. Make up a square follower board with rounded corners, and clamp it to the sander table. The follower board must be exactly located on the table, square to the disk and a set distance away from it. To figure out where to put the follower, measure the thickness of the pattern and of the sawn part, and subtract $1/16$ inch. This is the distance from the end of follower board to the sanding disk.

Feed the assembled pattern and part between the disk and the board fence. Except for finish sanding with the grain, this completes the outside of the curve.

Now you can use the completed outside of the curve as the pattern for band-sawing the inside. Remove the rail from the pattern, and scrape off the tape residue. Set the band-saw rip fence to the finished thickness of the rail, plus a bare $1/16$ inch for cleaning up. Now simply feed the workpiece through the band saw, with the outside of the curve bearing against the fence. The saw will follow this curve, creating a parallel inside surface.

The drum sander completes the inside surface, once again following the outside of the workpiece as a template. Set the distance between the sanding drum and the drill-press fence to the final thickness of the rail. Feed the rail past the drum, keeping the outside of the curve bearing against the fence. A final hand sanding completes the job.

STEP-BY-STEP: PATTERN CUTTING A CREST RAIL

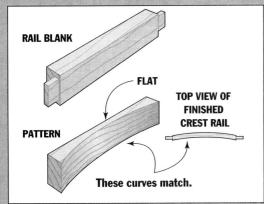

STEP 1 Cut the rail blanks to size and tenon them. Make a pattern of the rail's curve.

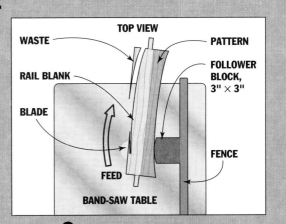

STEP 2 Stick the workpiece to the flat side of the pattern with double-sided carpet tape. Run the pattern against a curved follower block on the band saw to remove the bulk of the waste from the outside of the rail.

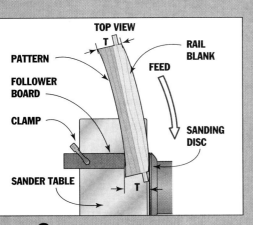

STEP 3 Clamp a follower board to the table of the disk sander. Feed the pattern and attached workpiece between the board fence and the sanding disk to complete the curve.

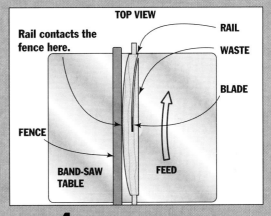

STEP 4 Remove the pattern, and cut the concave side of the curve on the band saw. The outside curve serves as a pattern against the fence.

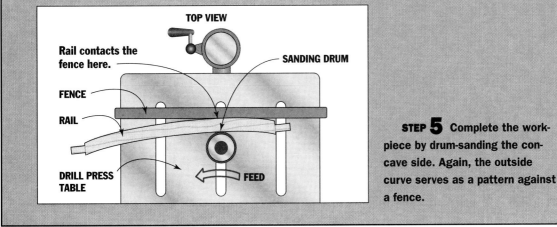

STEP 5 Complete the workpiece by drum-sanding the concave side. Again, the outside curve serves as a pattern against a fence.

Cutting Circles

Arcs and circles, unlike many curved shapes, can be shaped with a jig instead of from a pattern. The basic principle of the jig is to locate a pivot pin a set distance away from a cutter. To that end, I've seen a lot of infinitely adjustable circle-sawing jigs. In my opinion, they're more work than the problem is worth, since you'll never use most of the jig's adjustability.

It's a lot quicker to make a simple jig, as shown in *A Circle-Sawing Jig*, and set a new point in it for each radius you want to cut. The key is to make sure the center point is on a line perpendicular to the front of the teeth of the bandsaw blade. When you reach the size limits of the jig, it's no problem to make a bigger one, though you may have to support it on a high sawhorse. My general method for cutting circles is as follows:

STEP 1 Measure out from the blade to locate the center of the circle along the radius line. Drive a small brad into the jig to mark the center. Clip the head off the brad, leaving about ⅛ inch of metal exposed.

STEP 2 Locate the workpiece on the brad. Engage the runner in the miter gauge slot in the bandsaw table, start sawing, and advance the jig until the stop block hits the front of the table.

STEP 3 Pivot the workpiece on the brad to cut the circle, as shown in the photo.

STEP 4 Smooth the sawn edges by pivoting the disk against a belt, disk, or drum sander, using a similar jig as a guide.

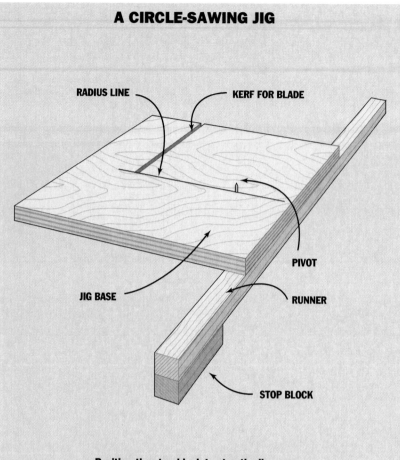

A CIRCLE-SAWING JIG

RADIUS LINE

KERF FOR BLADE

JIG BASE

PIVOT

RUNNER

STOP BLOCK

Position the stop block to stop the jig when the saw teeth meet the radius line.

A circular cut starts out as a straight line until the radius line reaches a point perpendicular to the front on the blade. When the jig's stop block hits the front of the table, you can start to pivot the workpiece.

Cutting Ellipses

An ellipse is essentially an elongated, or squashed, circle. As such, its form may be more in keeping with a design than a true circle's is. While an ellipse isn't as straightforward to make as a circle, it isn't as difficult as you might think. You may have seen a widget whimsically called a BS grinder or sometimes a

Washington shuttle. When you turn the crank, the blocks shuttle endlessly past one another, trapped in two perpendicular grooves. Since the end of the crank describes a true ellipse, clever woodworkers have made ellipse-routing jigs based on this device. Much as I admire their ingenuity, I don't actually have the patience to make such a jig.

I make ellipses the same way I make most other shapes, by constructing an accurate pattern against which to saw and rout the workpiece, as shown in *An Ellipse Pattern*. Since an ellipse is symmetrical on two axes, you only need to make a quarter-pattern. Always lay out the axes and draw the ellipse full size on the workpiece. There's no other way to orient the pattern accurately. Here's how to go about it:

STEP 1 Draw a rectangle as wide (A) and as high (B) as the ellipse you need. Divide the rectangle into quadrants.

STEP 2 Set two nails and a pencil through a hardwood stick, as shown in the drawing.

STEP 3 Stick a framing square on the axes of the ellipse with double-faced tape.

STEP 4 Keep the nails straddled tight across the framing square while you slide them along the blades. The pencil will trace out the ellipse, one quadrant at a time. Flip the square on the axes to draw the other quadrants.

STEP 5 When you have drawn the ellipse you want, make a quarter-pattern that fairs into tangents, as shown. Then you can pattern-cut the ellipse, one quarter at a time, as described in "Pattern Sawing" on page 38 and "Pattern Routing" on page 40.

AN ELLIPSE PATTERN

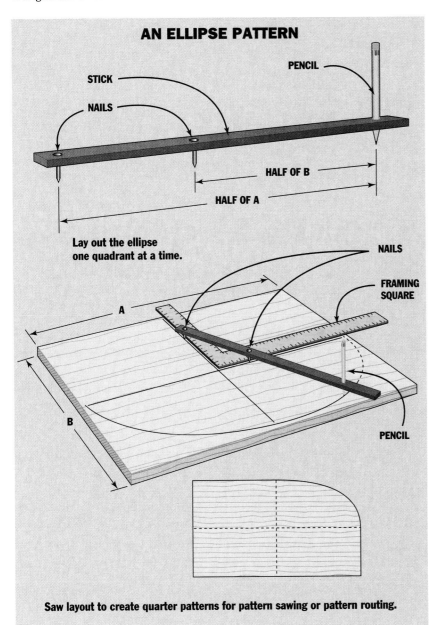

PENCIL

STICK

NAILS

HALF OF B

HALF OF A

Lay out the ellipse one quadrant at a time.

NAILS

FRAMING SQUARE

A

B

PENCIL

Saw layout to create quarter patterns for pattern sawing or pattern routing.

Shaping Gooseneck Moldings

Tall case clocks and highboy chests often have a sweeping gooseneck molding atop the bonnet. The traditional way of making this molding is to carve it with chisels and gouges. I prefer to cut such molding with a combination of pattern sawing, routing, and sanding.

Start by making an accurate half-pattern of the lower curve. Then use the half-pattern to create a full pattern, as shown in "Making a Gooseneck Molding." A full pattern is necessary because the two pieces of molding required are mirror images of each other and can't be made from a simple half pattern.

Attach the two workpieces to the full pattern with screws. Since the molding will be glued to the front of the cabinet, these screw holes will never show. Also, screw a strip of stock to the back edge of the full template for the straight molding you'll need on the cabinet sides. This serves two purposes. First, it keeps the pattern level on the router table when you run it. Second, it allows you to shape the straight molding with the same bit setups you'll use for the gooseneck.

Cut the molding to the general size and shape by pattern-sawing it, then rout it with a flush-trim bit to clean up the saw marks. Pattern-rout both the gooseneck and the straight stock to mold the edge. Depending on the profile and the bits you own, you can either guide the bit with a ball bearing or with a pointed follower as shown. With either system, the follower runs along the edge of

A sweeping gooseneck molding graces the bonnet of this tall case clock. Using a pattern jig, the straight molding on the bonnet sides was cut at the same time and to the same profile as the gooseneck.

the template. If you go with the pointed follower, you may need to relieve its underside to provide clearance for the bit. Start the cuts by pivoting the pattern against the

RIPPINGS

GETTING PATTERN CUTS UNDER CONTROL

When making patterns, always extend the curves beyond the finished ends of the workpiece. This way, you can engage the pattern with the follower before you actually start to cut away the workpiece itself, which gives you a lot more control over the operation.

starting pin. At some point, however, the pin may get in the way. If this occurs, remove the pin after the cut is underway.

Note that when routing the molding, part of the cut will be against the grain. You should be taking a small enough bite that you can climb-cut the uphill side of the curve without losing control. This (and sharp bits) will minimize tear-out.

Finally, separate the moldings from the template. Use the gooseneck's front face to pattern-saw and pattern-sand the parallel back edge. When using a point follower, be sure to keep the face of the template (or molding) perpendicular to the follower.

STEP-BY-STEP: MAKING A GOOSENECK MOLDING

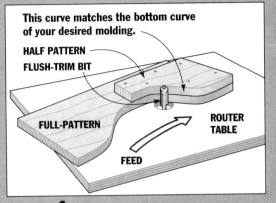

This curve matches the bottom curve of your desired molding.

HALF PATTERN
FLUSH-TRIM BIT
FULL-PATTERN
ROUTER TABLE
FEED

STEP 1 Make a full pattern for the molding from a half-pattern. Saw out the full-sized pattern, and smooth it with a flush-trim bit.

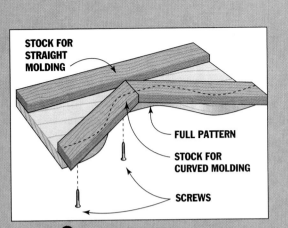

STOCK FOR STRAIGHT MOLDING
FULL PATTERN
STOCK FOR CURVED MOLDING
SCREWS

STEP 2 Attach the molding stock to the pattern. The grain of the gooseneck pieces runs more or less parallel to the pattern's edge.

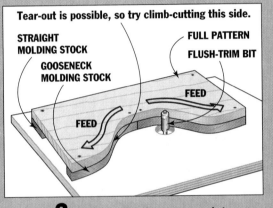

Tear-out is possible, so try climb-cutting this side.

STRAIGHT MOLDING STOCK
GOOSENECK MOLDING STOCK
FULL PATTERN
FLUSH-TRIM BIT
FEED
FEED

STEP 3 Pattern-saw the gooseneck to shape on the band saw. Then rout it flush to the pattern with a flush-trim bit.

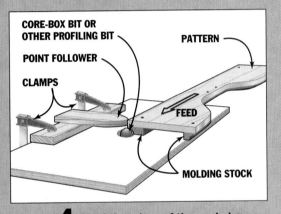

CORE-BOX BIT OR OTHER PROFILING BIT
POINT FOLLOWER
CLAMPS
PATTERN
FEED
MOLDING STOCK

STEP 4 Mold the edges of the workpieces. Depending on the profile you're after, you may need to use several different bits. A point follower guides the cut.

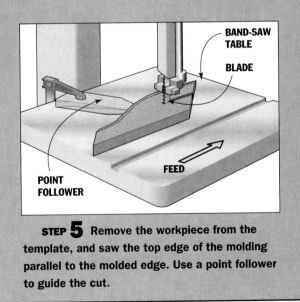

BAND-SAW TABLE
BLADE
FEED
POINT FOLLOWER

STEP 5 Remove the workpiece from the template, and saw the top edge of the molding parallel to the molded edge. Use a point follower to guide the cut.

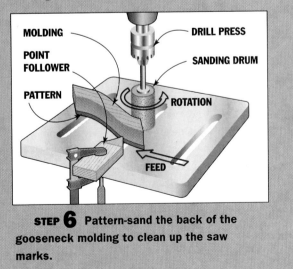

MOLDING
POINT FOLLOWER
PATTERN
DRILL PRESS
SANDING DRUM
ROTATION
FEED

STEP 6 Pattern-sand the back of the gooseneck molding to clean up the saw marks.

4

FRAME-AND-PANEL SHAPING

Key Ingredients

The frame and panel is an age-old solution to the problem of wood movement in solid construction. As shown in *Frame-and-Panel Construction*, the wide panel floats within a structural frame made from relatively narrow stock. The panel can then expand and contract freely while the dimensions of the frame remain constant.

Frame-and-panel construction can be used anywhere there's a need for large, solid-wood surfaces, like cabinet sides and backs, dust panels in chests of drawers, and especially doors. There are assorted ways to solve each half of the frame-and-panel puzzle, so it's useful to approach it as two distinct processes—first building the frame, then making the panel to fit the frame.

Making Frames

Traditionally, frames for raised panels were made with mortise-and-tenon joinery. This is still the most structurally sound approach if you're making a large frame or one that will get heavy use, like an entry door. However, when you make mortise-and-tenon doors, it is more difficult to add a profile to the inside edges of the frame. Techniques for doing that are shown in "Shaping a Mortise-

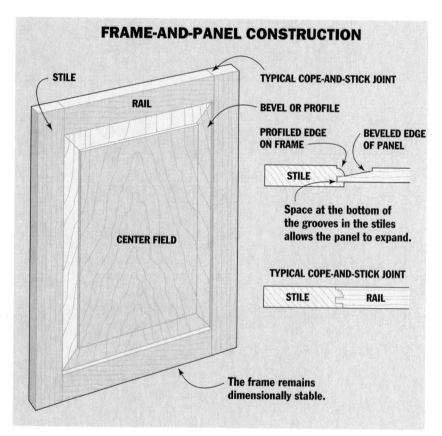

FRAME-AND-PANEL CONSTRUCTION

STILE

RAIL

CENTER FIELD

TYPICAL COPE-AND-STICK JOINT

BEVEL OR PROFILE

PROFILED EDGE ON FRAME

BEVELED EDGE OF PANEL

STILE

Space at the bottom of the grooves in the stiles allows the panel to expand.

TYPICAL COPE-AND-STICK JOINT

STILE   RAIL

The frame remains dimensionally stable.

and-Tenon Frame" on page 52.

For smaller, cabinet-sized frames and doors, cope-and-stick joints offer alternative to mortise-and-tenon construction. With cope-and-stick router bits or shaper cutters, you can cut the door joinery, the groove for the panel, and a molded profile around the inside edges of the frame parts in just a single pass. You end up with a short tongue-and-groove joint holding the frame together, supported by the mating

profiles of the cope-and-stick pattern itself; see *Cope-and-Stick Joinery*. The joint works flawlessly only if the parts match perfectly.

Raising Panels

Raising a panel by cutting a profile on its edges solves the problem of fitting a thick piece of wood into a narrow groove. The simplest approach is to taper the edges of the panel until they fit the groove. The taper can be made on just the front of the panel, or on both the front and back. As you can see in *Panel Profiles*, you can also create the effect of a raised panel simply by forming a tongue on the edge of the panel, leaving enough room for the panel to expand and contract. This is often referred to simply as a fielded panel. With a 1/4-inch gap, or reveal, around the field and shaped edges on both the panel and the frame edges, this is a simple way to set off a beautiful panel from its frame.

On old furniture, the bevel generally continues right off the edge of the panel. It doesn't flatten out to make a flat tongue. This is because the shapes were made with special panel-raising hand planes, as described in "Panel Raising with Hand Planes" on page 56.

Most panel-raising router bits and shaper cutters, on the other hand, automatically make a bevel that flows into a flat tongue. With this approach, the tongue

can be made to fit a little more snugly in the groove. Is one better than the other? I don't think so. It's a matter of what tools you happen to have and how much trouble you want to take. The panel will function just as well either way.

When it comes to raising panels, you have lots of choices. The shaper is the best machine for the job because it has the power to drive large cutters and the stability to produce a consistent cut. You can raise panels on the table saw, but the rough cut will need a good deal of sanding. If you have a powerful router, there are specialized router bits that do the job, including vertical panel raisers and "helicopter" bits. Or you can use standard router bits and customize the setup to make them cut the bevel you want. Finally, you can raise panels using specialized hand planes as well as standard bench planes plus a little help from the table saw or router bits.

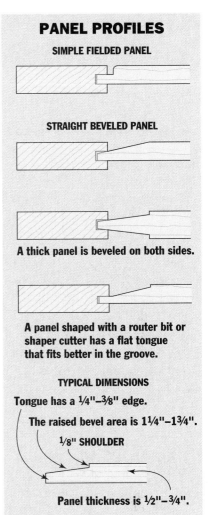

PANEL PROFILES

SIMPLE FIELDED PANEL

STRAIGHT BEVELED PANEL

A thick panel is beveled on both sides.

A panel shaped with a router bit or shaper cutter has a flat tongue that fits better in the groove.

TYPICAL DIMENSIONS
Tongue has a 1/4"–3/8" edge.
The raised bevel area is 1 1/4"–1 3/4".
1/8" SHOULDER
Panel thickness is 1/2"–3/4".

Whatever tool you choose, keep in mind that your stock must be straight and flat and that rails and stiles must be planed to the same thickness. These fundamentals are important when raising panels, but critical when making cope-and-stick frames. Any inaccuracies in your wood selection and preparation, as well as any wood distortion after you mill it, will result in faulty joints. Not only will your frame-and-panel constructions look shoddy, they might fall apart after a few years of service. Your only insurance is meticulous wood selection and careful preparation at the start.

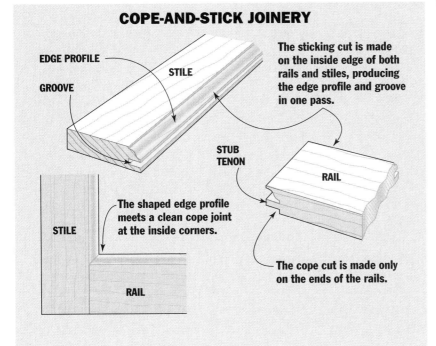

COPE-AND-STICK JOINERY

EDGE PROFILE
STILE
GROOVE

The sticking cut is made on the inside edge of both rails and stiles, producing the edge profile and groove in one pass.

STUB TENON

RAIL

The shaped edge profile meets a clean cope joint at the inside corners.

STILE

RAIL

The cope cut is made only on the ends of the rails.

Routing a Cope-and-Stick Joint

Cope-and-stick joints are a production solution to making perfectly matched profiles on the rails and stiles. The level of precision needed is found in heavyweight machines, which can make accurate cuts even on stock that's cupped or bowed slightly. You've probably heard of a double-end tenoner, which forms the cope profile on both ends of a rail while simultaneously cutting the tenons. Another machine, called a "sticker," shapes the matching counterprofile on the edges of rails and stiles.

A shaper is an ideal tool for both operations, because on it you can counter the problem of wood movement. A power stock feeder can hold the wood tight to the table when making the sticking cuts, and a sliding table with a hold-down clamp can do the same for the cope cut.

For a commercial operation, coping-and-sticking is extremely efficient because it permits continuous production of identical parts. Small shops have neither the tooling nor the overwhelming need to make this technique work flawlessly. Nevertheless, it's an interesting approach that can be fun to explore on the router table.

There are an assortment of router bits and shaper cutters designed for cutting cope-and-stick joinery. They all work the same way. In a nutshell, you rout a profile, which includes the panel groove, around the inside edges of the rails and stiles. This is called the sticking cut. Then you cut the exact counter profile, or cope cut,

into the ends of the rails.

The cope cut produces a short, "stub" tenon on the end of the rail that fits into the groove in the stile. (Refer to *Cope-and-Stick Joinery* on page 49.) This seems like a meager joint, but the profiled part of the joint provides good glue surface and it fits so well when properly cut that it adds considerable strength to the joint. It's plenty strong for cabinet doors, although you can't trust it for a thicker entry door that would undergo heavier stresses. For larger doors, use mortise-and-tenon joinery, then add the shaped edge treatment, as described in "Shaping a Mortise and Tenoned Frame." on page 52.

You need a strong router, at least 2 horsepower, and a sturdy router table to succeed with cope-and-stick cutters. Both cuts should be made in a single pass; making multiple passes will give you a

loose joint, and just a little loose is way too much with a cope-and-stick joint.

Cope-and-stick router cutters come in three configurations. The first uses two completely separate cutters, the second a single cutter that you raise and lower to form the separate cope-and-stick profiles, and the third has reversible cutters on a single shank. The set with two separate cutters allows you to work between two router tables, one setup to make the sticking cut, the other setup for the cope cut. If you happen to have two router tables, this is a nice arrangement. The height-adjustable cutter set is convenient. You set the fence, make one cut, then raise the cutter to make the second cut. However, when making one of the cuts, the entire bit is dangerously exposed above the table. The reversible sets require you to remove the cutter from the router, reverse the individual cutters on the shank, and then rechuck the assembly.

All these configurations work on the same principle: You make one of the cuts, then carefully set up the second cut to match, as shown in "Routing Cope-and-Stick Joints." When setting the second cut, use an extra piece of stock that was planed to the same thickness as the frame stock. Lay the two parts on a flat surface to test the fit. Shift the cutters up or down by minute amounts until the two parts fit perfectly. When using cope-and-stick cutters, there are a few subtleties to keep in mind that will help you get good results:

● Although cope-and-stick cutters are designed for $\frac{3}{4}$-inch-thick stock, you'll get better results with $\frac{13}{16}$-inch-thick stock. The added thickness creates a beefier lip of wood at the back of the groove. The thinner this lip is, the more likely it is to split or crack.

- Keep the opening in the router table fence as narrow as possible so your stock is supported close to the cutter. This is especially important with the cope cut, so the end of a rail doesn't tip into the cutter.

- When making the sticking cut, you can use fingerboards to hold the stock tight against both the fence and the table. Fingerboards are definitely worthwhile if you're making the sticking cut on long lengths of stock that will be crosscut later. When you make the cope cut, however, fingerboards are likely to cause trouble, not prevent it. Because it's a short, end-grain cut, you can make it with firm hand pressure holding the stock down and in.

- When you make the cope cuts on the ends of the rails, you must use a backer board, as shown in **STEP 2** and **3**, to keep the rails square to the fence and to prevent tear-out on the back edge of the rails. When you cut the first end of each rail, the unprofiled edge of the rail must be against the backer board. When you go to cut the other end of the rails, the profiled edge will face the backer board. If you make the cut this way, the profiled edge will tear out because it's unsupported. To prevent this, cope one edge of the backer board, then flip it over so it mates with the profiled edge of the rails, as shown in **STEP 3**. Then make all the second cope cuts.

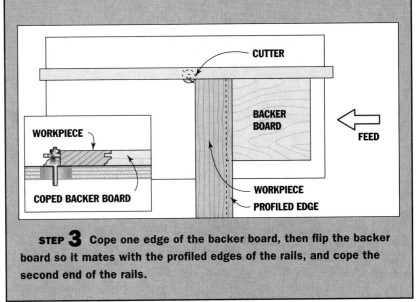

STEP BY STEP: ROUTING COPE AND STICK JOINTS

Hand pressure or finger board holds stock tight against table.

FEED

Hand pressure holds stock tight against fence.

REVERSIBLE COPE-AND-STICK CUTTER

STEP 1 Cut the sticking profile on the inside edge of all the rails and stiles.

10"

10"

FEED

PROFILED EDGE   **SQUARE BACKER BOARD**

STEP 2 After cutting the rails to length, make the cope cut on one end of all the rails.

CUTTER

BACKER BOARD

FEED

WORKPIECE

COPED BACKER BOARD

WORKPIECE

PROFILED EDGE

STEP 3 Cope one edge of the backer board, then flip the backer board so it mates with the profiled edges of the rails, and cope the second end of the rails.

SHAPING A MORTISE-AND-TENON FRAME

When making frame-and-panel doors, you can either leave the frame stock square or add a profile to its inside edges, adding a bit of visual interest. There are two ways to add the profile: Either "plant" loose moldings, or shape the frame and miter the shaped parts.

Using Planted Moldings

This is the least complicated approach because the square edges of the frame stock remain intact. In fact, you assemble the frame without worrying about the panels. Then you "plant" strips of mitered molding around the inside edges of the frame, using glue and/or nails. First attach the moldings to one side of the frame, then set the panel against the planted moldings. Finally plant the moldings around the other side of the frame to lock the panel in place, as shown in "Applying Planted Moldings."

You can use any profile for the planted molding. The molding can sit completely within the frame edge, or it can have a rabbet that wraps the edge of the frame, as shown in *Planted Moldings*. Because it's such a small strip of wood, you'll want to rip it from a wider piece of stock. You can miter the molding on the table saw or with a chop saw. For a single frame, work in sequence around the opening, installing one piece, then measuring the adjacent piece. For multiple frames using the same dimensions, set up stops on the saw fence to speed the work.

PLANTED MOLDINGS

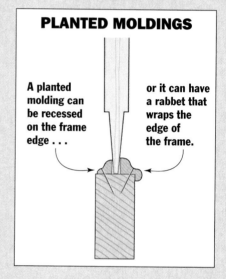

A planted molding can be recessed on the frame edge . . .

or it can have a rabbet that wraps the edge of the frame.

STEP BY STEP: APPLYING PLANTED MOLDINGS

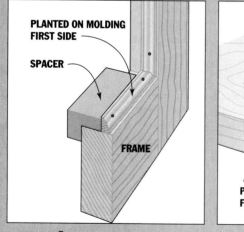

PLANTED ON MOLDING FIRST SIDE

SPACER

FRAME

STEP 1 Plant the molding on first side of frame, using a spacer to locate it. Secure the molding with brads or glue, or both.

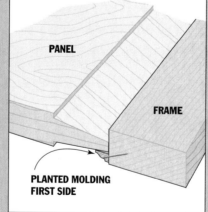

PANEL

FRAME

PLANTED MOLDING FIRST SIDE

STEP 2 Lay the frame flat and set the panel in place against the planted molding.

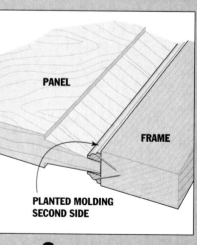

PANEL

FRAME

PLANTED MOLDING SECOND SIDE

STEP 3 Plant the molding on the second side of the frame to trap the panel in place.

Mitering a Shaped Frame

An alternative to planting separate moldings around a frame is to shape it right on the frame stock. With this approach, you cut the mortise-and-tenon joinery, then rout a groove for the panel, and cut a profile along all the inside edges of the frame pieces. To bring the molded edges together at the inside corners, you have to miter the molding on the ends of the rails, and you have to both miter it and cut away the excess on the stiles, as shown in "Mitering a Beaded Frame."

The advantage of this technique is that you don't have to deal with a bunch of loose strips of molding. You also don't have to be concerned about the molding matching the frame in color or grain. However, you still have to cut miters at each of the joints. And if you don't get one right, you either have to live with a poor miter, or remake the rail or stile completely.

To set up the table saw for mitering the profile, first crank the blade to 45 degrees, and use a scrap piece of stock to set the blade height. It should just barely nip the shoulder of the profile. Then set the fence, using the length of the tenon on one of the rails as a guide. The end of the tenon will butt against the fence as the miter gauge guides the stock through the cut. Cut the test miter, then make all the rail miters before moving on to the next setup.

Reset the fence for the miters on the stiles, again using a scrap of shaped stock. Here, the ends of the stiles butt against the fence.

Again, cut a trial miter on scrap stock, then check the fit against a completed mitered rail. Once the setup is right, miter all the stiles.

At this stage the mitered parts won't fit together completely because the profile on the stile is in the way. To cut away this waste on the stiles, use the band saw with a fence to guide the cut and a stop to end the cut. Don't try to band-saw right to the shoulder of the profile. If you cut too deeply, you'll damage the shoulder of the joint. Instead, leave about 1/16 inch of waste on the shoulder, and use the router table setup shown in **STEP 3** to trim it clean. Use the widest straight bit you have. A hinge-mortising bit is designed for this kind of shallow, bottom-cleaning cut.

STEP BY STEP: MITERING A BEADED FRAME

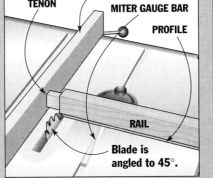

STEP 1 Miter the ends of the rails. Guide the stock through the cut with the miter gauge. Set the rip fence to locate the cut.

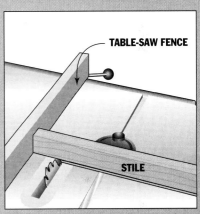

STEP 2 Reset the fence and cut the miters on the stiles.

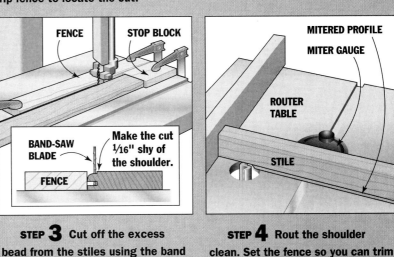

STEP 3 Cut off the excess bead from the stiles using the band saw, with a fence and a stop.

STEP 4 Rout the shoulder clean. Set the fence so you can trim right up to the base of the miter.

Panel Raising on the Router Table

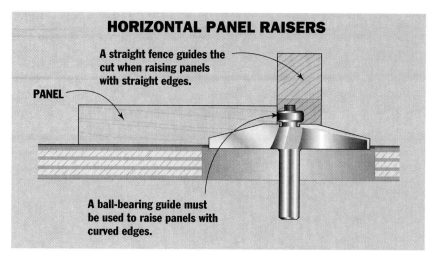

HORIZONTAL PANEL RAISERS

A straight fence guides the cut when raising panels with straight edges.

PANEL

A ball-bearing guide must be used to raise panels with curved edges.

When raising panels on the router table, you have two specialty bit choices: the horizontal bit and the vertical bit. Horizontal bits, sometimes called "helicopter" bits, are typically a huge 3 inches in diameter. A bit this big exerts tremendous force on the router when it's run at the tool's full speed of 22,000 rpm. Most manufacturers recommend slowing the router to half that speed. At this slower speed, a horizontal bit requires a lot of power. So you need a powerful router, 2 horsepower or better, with speed control. Even then you'll want to make a series of passes to reach the full depth of cut. The chief advantage of horizontal panel raisers is that you cut with the panels flat on the table, as shown in *Horizontal Panel Raisers*. A second advantage is

that they typically have a ball-bearing pilot, so they can follow the edge of a curved panel.

Vertical bits have relatively small diameters and can be run at full router speeds of 22,000 rpms. However, you need to stand your panels on edge and run them vertically past the bit. This is more challenging than laying them flat, but by using a tall fence and taking a series of light cuts, it's not a difficult operation. See *Vertical Panel Raisers*.

Vertical panel raisers are not useful for raising curved-panel edges.

No matter which version of the panel-raising bit you use, there are a few basic rules to follow:

- Make sure the panel is well supported close to the bit. This means cutting an opening in the fence that is just slightly larger than the bit itself and reducing the opening in the router table if possible. If your router table opening is too large, add an auxiliary table surface, as described on page 25.
- Fingerboards are really not necessary with panel-raising bits. For one thing, the cutter is always buried under the panel, so your hands are safe. Also, fingerboards tend to cause divots at the beginning and end of the cut. That's not a problem with other shaping cuts when you can leave the stock long to account for the divots, but you can't do that with raised panels because they are already cut to final dimensions.
- Raise the panel in a series of light passes, with the final one being just a skim cut. Even with this approach, the profile won't always meet perfectly at the corners. Assume that you'll need to blend the profile at

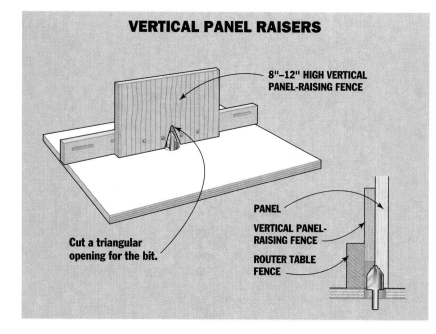

VERTICAL PANEL RAISERS

8"–12" HIGH VERTICAL PANEL-RAISING FENCE

Cut a triangular opening for the bit.

PANEL

VERTICAL PANEL-RAISING FENCE

ROUTER TABLE FENCE

some of the corners with hand tools and sandpaper.

● Rout the ends of the panels before the sides. That will eliminate any end-grain tear-out at the corners.

Another way to rout raised panels is to cut the bevel with a combination of general-purpose bits. The idea is to make a series of separate cuts to define the parts of the raised panel instead of making the full profile with a single bit.

It's easy to make a continuous bevel, but you'll have to experiment to make a smooth transition to a flat tongue. You do need to make a tilted auxiliary fence for the router table, with a tilt angle that matches the bevel angle you want, as shown in *Panel-Raising Fence for the Router Table*. You probably could design an adjustable-angle fence, but I wouldn't because the fence really needs to be solid and vibration free.

This fence is angled at 80 degrees to the router table, for a

10-degree bevel angle. A smaller angle creates a longer bevel, too long for the bit to make the cut. You can increase the bevel angle a few degrees. However, the steeper the angle, the shorter the bevel, and the more difficult it is to fit the panel in its groove. A steeper bevel also increases the risk of the panel splitting the groove.

Make a kerf-cut on the table saw to define the raised field. A sharp cross-cut blade will leave a clean, crisp shoulder. You could also create a coved shoulder with a ¼-inch core-box bit in the router table, as shown in **STEP 1** in "Panel Raising with Straight Bits."

If you want to make a tongue, instead of continuous bevel, rout that first. When you cut the bevel, you'll need to blend the point where the tongue and the bevel meet with hand planes, or else accept the small step as an intended feature, as shown in **STEP 3**.

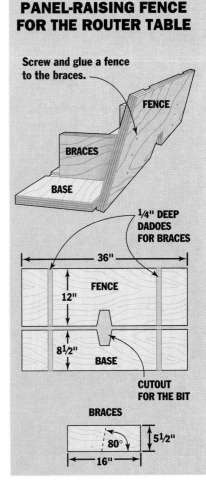

PANEL-RAISING FENCE FOR THE ROUTER TABLE

Screw and glue a fence to the braces.

FENCE

BRACES

BASE

¼" DEEP DADOES FOR BRACES

36"

12"

FENCE

8½"

BASE

CUTOUT FOR THE BIT

BRACES

80°

5½"

16"

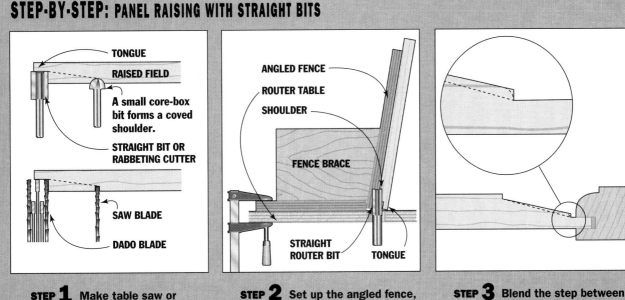

STEP-BY-STEP: PANEL RAISING WITH STRAIGHT BITS

TONGUE

RAISED FIELD

A small core-box bit forms a coved shoulder.

STRAIGHT BIT OR RABBETING CUTTER

SAW BLADE

DADO BLADE

ANGLED FENCE

ROUTER TABLE

SHOULDER

FENCE BRACE

STRAIGHT ROUTER BIT

TONGUE

STEP 1 Make table saw or router cuts to define the raised field and the tongue.

STEP 2 Set up the angled fence, and make the bevel cuts with a straight bit.

STEP 3 Blend the step between the bevel and tongue by planing, sanding, or rounding over the corner.

Panel Raising on the Table Saw

You can raise a straight-beveled panel entirely on the table saw. The table-saw method is essentially the same as routing with a straight cutter, except that you need a high vertical fence that's perpendicular to the saw table, and you tilt the saw arbor to get the bevel angle. You can cut a straight bevel or a bevel that ends in a flat tongue. If you choose the second option, saw the tongue first. Start with the shoulder cut that defines the raised field, as shown in "Table-Saw Panel Raising."

As you saw the panels, keep these other points in mind:

● Screw a high auxiliary fence onto the saw's rip fence. Tilt the saw blade to the desired bevel angle, and set up a fingerboard to press the panel tightly against the fence right over the sawblade. Note that the fingerboard needs to be elevated above the height of the blade.

● Determine the bevel angle by finding the panel's edge thickness. If you'll be cutting a tongue, it will match the width of the groove. A straight-beveled panel should be slightly thinner at its edge than the groove so it can fit into the groove to a depth of $\frac{1}{4}$ inch to $\frac{3}{8}$ inch. Decide on the width of the bevel and the depth of the shoulder. Connecting the shoulder to the edge of the panel gives you the bevel angle.

● A bevel angle of 10 degrees is about right. You can go a few degrees on either side of this without any problems.

● Always work with the back of the

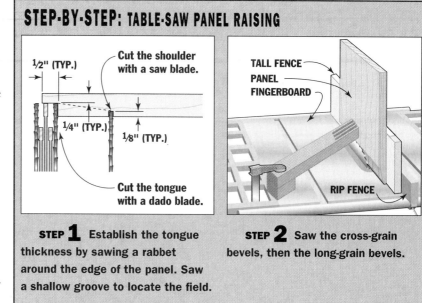

STEP-BY-STEP: TABLE-SAW PANEL RAISING

1/2" (TYP.)
Cut the shoulder with a saw blade.
1/4" (TYP.)
1/8" (TYP.)
Cut the tongue with a dado blade.

STEP 1 Establish the tongue thickness by sawing a rabbet around the edge of the panel. Saw a shallow groove to locate the field.

TALL FENCE
PANEL
FINGERBOARD
RIP FENCE

STEP 2 Saw the cross-grain bevels, then the long-grain bevels.

panel against the high fence. This may mean working with the fence on the left side of the blade instead of on the right, depending on which way your blade tilts. If this technique is new for you, go through the motions of the cut with the motor off to get a feel for the difference.

● This is a deep cut, so use a sharp rip blade. Make the cut in two passes, first cutting most of the waste off, then readjusting the fence for a light finishing cut. If the saw labors or the wood burns, change to a rip blade with fewer teeth. In this situation, a sharp steel rip blade may give a cleaner result than a carbide blade. Or try setting the fence just shy of the full depth of cut, and then raise the blade in increments until it reaches the shoulder. Finally, adjust the fence to take a light cut off the whole bevel.

● Bevel the ends of the panels first so any tear-out will be eliminated when you bevel the sides.

Panel Raising with Hand Planes

In the old days woodworkers had only one technique for raising panels: They hand cut them with special planes. You might find one of these planes among the old tools at a flea market. Or you can buy a new one, though they cost a small fortune. The sequence for using one is shown in "Hand-Tool Panel Raising."

Without a panel plane, you can nonetheless raise an acceptable panel using ordinary bench planes. Getting a clean shoulder is the most difficult part of raising panels by hand, and for that you need a shoulder or rabbet plane. But there's no reason to be a purist about it. You can always cut the shoulder and tongue on the table saw or router table, then remove the waste and clean up the bevel with your bench planes. Plane cross grain before planing long grain. That way cross-grain tear-out at the corners will be removed by the long grain cuts. Clean up with a block plane held askew to the edge of the panel.

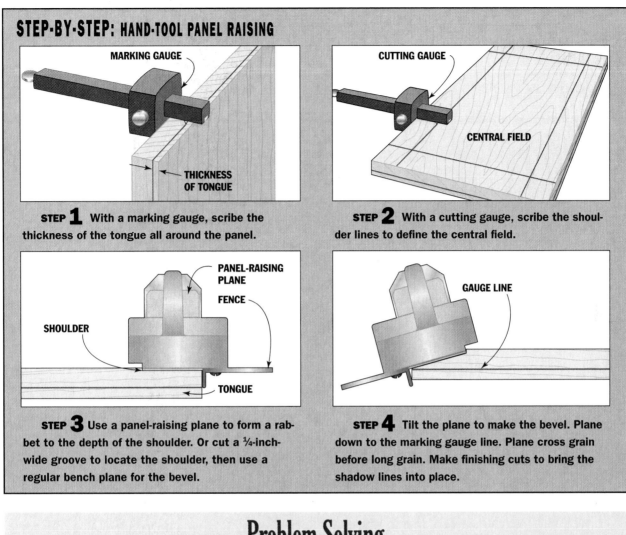

STEP-BY-STEP: HAND-TOOL PANEL RAISING

STEP 1 With a marking gauge, scribe the thickness of the tongue all around the panel.

STEP 2 With a cutting gauge, scribe the shoulder lines to define the central field.

STEP 3 Use a panel-raising plane to form a rabbet to the depth of the shoulder. Or cut a ¼-inch-wide groove to locate the shoulder, then use a regular bench plane for the bevel.

STEP 4 Tilt the plane to make the bevel. Plane down to the marking gauge line. Plane cross grain before long grain. Make finishing cuts to bring the shadow lines into place.

Problem Solving
Dealing with Loose Panels

Fitting a panel into a frame is close tolerance woodworking. No matter how careful you are, sometimes you make the bevel or tongue too thin, or the panel too narrow, and end up with a poor fit.

PROBLEM	SOLUTION
One bevel on a pair of book-matched panels is gouged by the router bit.	Salvage the panels by trimming one edge on each, and re-beveling it. Make new rails and stiles slightly wider to make up for the reduced size of the panels.
A panel is a bit narrow and is likely to open a gap when it shrinks.	Pin the panel in place so it can't shift. Predrill and insert a small dowel at the center of the rails (but not the stiles) into the edge of the panel. Trim off the excess dowel length with a sharp chisel.
A panel rattles when you open or close the door.	Squeeze a dab of clear silicone caulk into the groove at the center of each rail and stile on the inside of the door. The silicone will keep the panel from rattling, but it's flexible enough to allow normal expansion and contraction.

PUSHING THE LIMITS: Making an Arch-Top Panel

By adding an arch top to a raised panel door, you'll turn an ordinary piece of work into a distinctive one. The arch-top door descends from the arched opening of classical architecture, and it has, to many people, an air of perfection.

The curve of an arch-top cabinet door should be smooth and symmetrical, with the curve of the rail echoing that of the panel, as shown in the photo.

An arch-top panel door has a molded frame as well as a shaped and molded panel.

To make a well-built arch-top door, you have to solve the problem of making curved parts that fit together on a curved line. The answer is to pattern-rout the pieces. Pattern routing is the process of making a pattern and then using the pattern to make exact duplicates. Related techniques like pattern sawing on the band saw and pattern sanding also come into play here. All of these techniques are covered in detail in Chapter 3, so here we'll concentrate on the door itself.

Making the Jig

Since the panel will be what people see, its curve is the one that must be right. First, make a full-size drawing of the arch to work out a smooth, symmetrical curve. Next, make a half-pattern by dividing the drawing on its center line, then tracing the half-curve onto graph paper. Extend the curve about 2 inches past the outside edge and center line, as shown in *Half-Pattern Jig*. These sections of the template act like runways for the router bit to start and end the cut. Cut out the paper pattern and glue it

onto ½-inch plywood. Band-saw the plywood half-pattern, and sand it smooth.

To complete the jig, screw the half-pattern to a solid wood edge guide, as shown. The edge guide should be a few inches longer than your longest panel to allow room for a stop block. Note that when using the jig you have to work from both sides of the panel.

Making the Panel

To make the arch, first fit the jig onto your panel stock, and trace half the curve, as shown in **STEP 1** in "Making an Arch-Top Panel Door." Tilt your pencil just a bit, so the line is about ¹⁄₁₆ inch away from the pattern's edge. That way when you saw the curve, you'll be safely proud of the actual finished edge. Next, flip the panel over, fit the jig to its other edge, and draw the other half of the curve.

Band-saw the panel, as shown in **STEP 2**. Stay on the waste side of the line. Saw to the top of the arch from one side, then flip the panel over and saw the other half. Minor

---

STEP-BY-STEP: MAKING AN ARCH-TOP PANEL DOOR

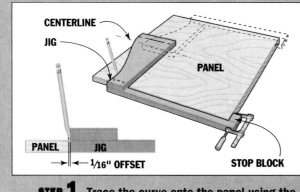

CENTERLINE
JIG
PANEL
PANEL   JIG
1/16" OFFSET
STOP BLOCK

STEP 1 Trace the curve onto the panel using the half-pattern jig. Mark one half of the curve on the front and mark the other half on the back.

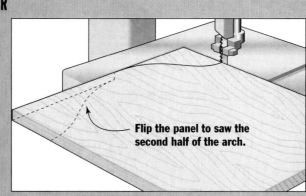

Flip the panel to saw the second half of the arch.

STEP 2 Band-saw one half of the curve, then flip the panel, and band-saw the other half.

variations don't matter because this step is just to remove most of the waste before routing. Use the first panel to lay out all of the subsequent panels—it's faster than using the jig.

Now, clamp the panel into the jig, as shown in **STEP 3**. Mount a flush-trim bit in your table-mounted router. Hold the edge of the panel against a starting pin to start the cut, and follow the pattern from the edge to just past the center line. Remove the jig, flip the panel over, reclamp the jig to the panel, and rout the other half of the curve. The curve should be smooth, but there'll probably be a bump at the center line where the two saw cuts meet. Sand off this bump, or you'll faithfully reproduce it when you raise the panel.

Raising the Panel

Mount a horizontal panel raiser in the router so it sits just above the surface of the baseplate, as shown in **STEP 4**. Then add an auxiliary tabletop of ½-inch plywood. Cut a wide slot in the back edge to fit around the cutter, as shown. This setup reduces the router's vertical reach by the thickness of the plywood, but you don't need much reach.

Raise the cutter about ⅛ inch above the surface of the auxiliary top. Use the starting pin to begin in the middle of a long side of the panel, and rout all the way around.

Make a series of light passes, raising the cutter about ¹⁄₁₆ inch at a time. After each pass, check the edge of the panel against the groove in the frame until it fits.

Make the last cut as clean as possible. Turn the router speed up to about 15,000 rpm, and raise the cutter by just a tiny amount, less than ¹⁄₆₄ inch. The purpose of this final pass is to skim off torn grain, not to remove any material.

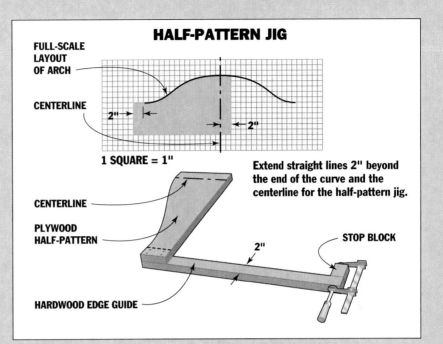

HALF-PATTERN JIG

FULL-SCALE LAYOUT OF ARCH

CENTERLINE

2"

2"

1 SQUARE = 1"

Extend straight lines 2" beyond the end of the curve and the centerline for the half-pattern jig.

CENTERLINE

PLYWOOD HALF-PATTERN

STOP BLOCK

2"

HARDWOOD EDGE GUIDE

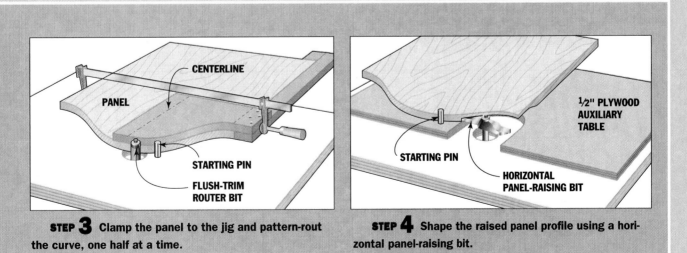

STEP **3** Clamp the panel to the jig and pattern-rout the curve, one half at a time.

CENTERLINE

PANEL

STARTING PIN

FLUSH-TRIM ROUTER BIT

STARTING PIN

HORIZONTAL PANEL-RAISING BIT

½" PLYWOOD AUXILIARY TABLE

STEP **4** Shape the raised panel profile using a horizontal panel-raising bit.

PUSHING THE LIMITS: Making a Curved Door Rail

Making a curved rail is a three-step process. First, make the rail as a rectangular, square-edged blank, and cut the cope profile in the ends of the rails while the blank is still square. Second, shape the rail blank to match the arched profile on the panel. For this you'll need to make a sandwich jig or a half-pattern jig. Third, cut the sticking pattern on the curved rail.

Grain direction is a problem when shaping the edge of a curved rail. The bit cuts uphill against the grain on one side of the curve and is likely to tear the wood up. The solution is to make a two-sided sandwich jig, starting from the half-pattern on the panel-raising jig shown in *Half-Pattern Jig* on page 59. Like the half-pattern jig, the sandwich jig allows you to shape half of the edge from one side and the other half from the second side.

Making the Sandwich Jig

To make the sandwich jig, saw two blanks from ¾-inch-hardwood plywood or medium-density fiber-

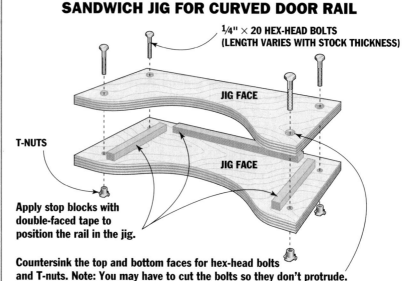

SANDWICH JIG FOR CURVED DOOR RAIL

¼" × 20 HEX-HEAD BOLTS (LENGTH VARIES WITH STOCK THICKNESS)

JIG FACE

T-NUTS

JIG FACE

Apply stop blocks with double-faced tape to position the rail in the jig.

Countersink the top and bottom faces for hex-head bolts and T-nuts. Note: You may have to cut the bolts so they don't protrude.

board (MDF). Trace the entire panel curve onto both blanks. Band-saw one of them to the line and drum-sand it smooth. This completes one part of the sandwich jig.

Band-saw the other part about ¹⁄₁₆-inch outside the pencil line. Mark the centerline on both pieces. Tape the two pieces together with double-sided carpet tape, and use the ½-inch straight cutter with the

ball-bearing pilot to trim the second band-sawn edge exactly to the sanded one. Clamp the two parts together with the curved edges aligned. Drill and countersink the outside faces of the blanks for ¼-inch × 20 machine bolts and T-nuts. The hex heads and the T-nuts must be recessed slightly into the faces of the jig. You may have to cut the bolts, depending on the thick-

STEP-BY-STEP: SHAPING THE CURVED RAIL

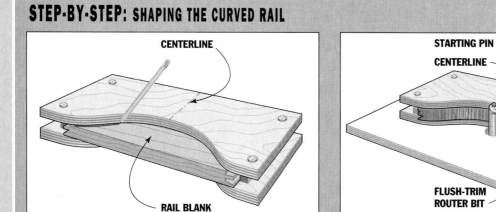

CENTERLINE

RAIL BLANK

STARTING PIN

CENTERLINE

FLUSH-TRIM ROUTER BIT

STEP 1 Position the rail blank in the sandwich jig, and trace the curve onto it. Then remove the blank from the jig, and rough-cut the waste on the band saw.

STEP 2 Mount the blank in the jig, and pattern-rout one half of the rail blank, working from the end to the center. Flip over the blank to trim the other half.

The starting pin helps you ease into the sticking cut. Bring the workpiece up to the pin, then pivot on the pin until the bearing rides the edge of the rail.

The starting pin also helps you stop the cut. Pivot the workpiece from the bearing onto the pin and away from the cutter.

(See "Pattern Routing" on page 40 for more on sandwich jigs.)

Shaping the Rail

With the sandwich jig made, the first step is to rough out the rail as shown in **STEP 1** of "Shaping the Curved Rail." Cross cut the rails to final length, set a rail blank in the jig, and trace the curve onto the blank. Remove the blank and saw off the waste on the band saw. Now bolt the sawn blank into the sandwich jig, and smooth the edge by routing with a ½-inch flush-trim bit. To avoid tear-out, rout downhill (with the grain) from one end of the blank to the centerline, then turn the jig over to rout down from the other end, as shown in **STEP 2**.

Any imperfections in the shaped edge will be transferred to the sticking cut in the next step, so sand the rail smooth now. A drum sander in the drill press works well.

The last step is to shape the edges of all the frame members with the sticking cut, using a cope-and-stick cutter. To shape the

ness of your rails, so they don't protrude. (Here's a tip: If you hammer the ⁷⁄₁₆-inch hex head of a ¼-inch bolt into a ²⁹⁄₆₄-inch countersunk hole, it'll lock tight.) Stick stop blocks to the jig with double-sided tape to position the rail, as shown in *Sandwich Jig for Curved Door Rail*.

curved rail, you have to use the cutter's bearing to guide the cut. Set up the cutter, as described in "Routing a Cope-and-Stick Joint" on page 50.

You also need to use a starting pin to begin and end the cut, as shown in **STEP 3** and **STEP 4** and the photos above.

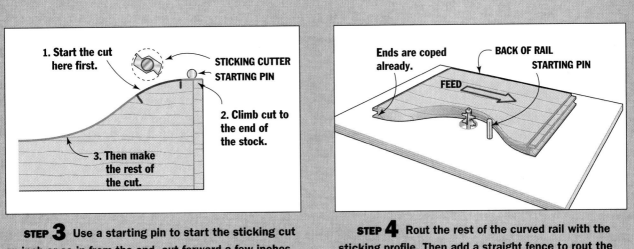

1. Start the cut here first.

STICKING CUTTER
STARTING PIN

2. Climb cut to the end of the stock.

3. Then make the rest of the cut.

Ends are coped already.

BACK OF RAIL
STARTING PIN

FEED

STEP 3 Use a starting pin to start the sticking cut an inch or so in from the end, cut forward a few inches, then climb-cut to the end.

STEP 4 Rout the rest of the curved rail with the sticking profile. Then add a straight fence to rout the profile on the bottom rail and the stiles.

5

SHAPING SURFACES AND THREE-DIMENSIONAL PIECES

Key Ingredients

Until this point, I've dealt with shaping and profiling in terms of lines and cutouts, where the workpiece isn't too far removed from a straight stick or board. Another realm of possibilities opens up when you think about shaping pieces in three dimensions, moving away from flat and parallel.

This kind of work can range from complex and precise to simple and rough, from producing a set of cabriole legs for a suite of dining chairs to chopping out a dough bowl from half a log. In between are techniques such as cutting tapers, making dowels, and shaping such contours as the chair seat shown in the photo above at right.

Linear shapes like tapers and dowels lend themselves well to jigs and machine work. Less regimented shapes, like curved legs or contoured chair seats, rely on a blend of hand and machine work. While the techniques are all interrelated, there are no hard and fast rules for what it takes to produce any given shape. Quite often, you have to combine

Making a comfortable wooden chair seat requires shaping a piece of wood to fit the contours of the human body. Traditional chair seats were carved from softer woods such as pine and poplar. These woods are easier to work than harder species.

techniques to get the result you want. This experimentation is one of the things about woodworking that I enjoy the most.

When you give up flat, parallel surfaces and edges, your work becomes more complicated because it is harder to find reference surfaces from which to measure. How to hold onto the workpiece also becomes an issue because it is often difficult to find a way to clamp an irregular shape. Good

planning can help you overcome these obstacles. As a general rule, you should make joints first, while the workpiece is still square, leaving shaping and contouring to do as a final step.

When you get to shaping, you have to study how the wood grain runs through your workpiece. Wood is a three-dimensional matrix of fibers, which always must be cut downhill. Cut uphill, and the wood will tear out.

Routing a Surface

You can use a router to shape the entire surface of a board. With this technique, you can flatten large or irregular pieces that you can't surface in your regular manner. It's slow-going, so the technique is no substitute for jointing and planing. But the router can put a flat surface on badly twisted planks, on end grain, and on large slabs of wood.

As shown in the photo below, the idea is to block the workpiece up level and stable on top of the workbench, and to flank it with two parallel rails. Mount the router on a carriage or sled that rides atop the rails, as shown in *Router Sled*. Some people make a permanent jig for this kind of work, but I've always found each

For special applications, you can use your router to flatten wood. Work the router sled back and forth across the slab of wood, removing no more than ⅛ inch with each pass. The surface won't be perfect, but it will be within range of hand planing and sanding.

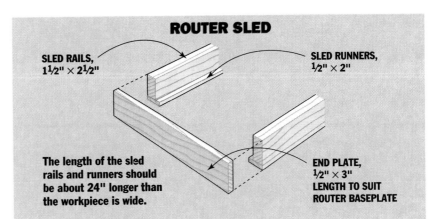

ROUTER SLED

SLED RAILS,
1½" × 2½"

SLED RUNNERS,
½" × 2"

The length of the sled rails and runners should be about 24" longer than the workpiece is wide.

END PLATE,
½" × 3"
LENGTH TO SUIT
ROUTER BASEPLATE

situation to be different enough that the "universal" jig can't quite handle it. So I keep the traveling sled, but I set up new rails each time around. Most of the time, a pair of straight 2 × 4s will do the job. They need to extend a foot beyond the workpiece at each end to support the sled at the ends of the cut. The regular dog system on the workbench will grab most slabs of wood. Add blocks and wedges underneath the slab to keep it from rocking.

Fit your router with an auxiliary baseplate so it sits easily in the sled. The width of the baseplate determines the inside width of the sled.

The bit that works best with this setup is a ¾-inch-diameter bottoming bit—the kind sold to clean up the bottom of a dado. It is designed to cut with its end rather than its side, so it leaves a cleaner surface. A core-box bit also works, though it leaves a rougher surface.

A similar setup can help you rout a contoured surface such as a chair seat or bench seat. Cut a pair of rails to the contour you want, as shown in *Routing a Contoured Surface*. You'll need to experiment with the shape of the rails because the path the bit follows won't exactly match the rail curve. For curved work, a core-box bit works better than the bottoming bit because it has no corners to dig in.

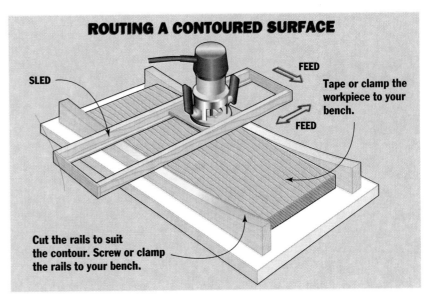

ROUTING A CONTOURED SURFACE

SLED

FEED

FEED

Tape or clamp the workpiece to your bench.

Cut the rails to suit the contour. Screw or clamp the rails to your bench.

Cove Cutting

Cutting coves on the table saw is a trick that isn't all that obvious at first. It's easy and the results are excellent. It involves running the workpiece across the saw table at an angle, as shown in the photo below. A shallow angle (close to parallel to the rip fence) produces a narrow cove, while a steep angle produces a wide one. You control the depth of the cut by adjusting the blade height. The limiting factor is the diameter of the saw blade.

You can saw coves with a combination blade, although the type of blade you choose isn't that important. The cut is in between a rip and a crosscut, so no matter what blade you use, you'll still have a fair amount of cleanup.

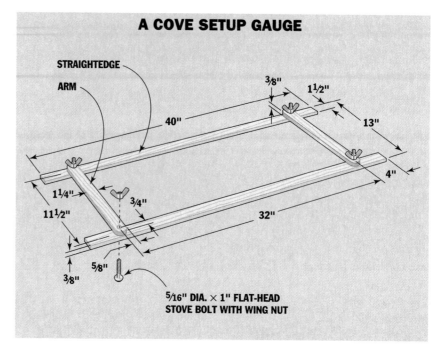

A COVE SETUP GAUGE

STRAIGHTEDGE

ARM

40"

3/8"   1 1/2"

13"

4"

1 1/4"

3/4"

11 1/2"

32"

3/8"

5/8"

5/16" DIA. × 1" FLAT-HEAD
STOVE BOLT WITH WING NUT

You'll be surprised at how well cove cutting on the table saw works. In fact, it only counts as advanced the first time you try it. After that, it's easy.

You'll get much cleaner results from 1-inch bullnose cutters in a table-saw molding head. This wide cutter produces light fluffy shavings, leaving a smooth surface behind. While the molding head won't cut as wide or as deep a cove as a regular saw blade, it will probably handle 98 percent of the coves you'll ever need. (For more on table-saw molding heads, see "Shaping with a Table-Saw Molding Head" on page 78.)

Set up your saw to cove as shown in "Cove Cutting on the Table Saw." To make setting up the fence on the saw easier, make up a parallel rule, as shown in *A Cove Setup Gauge*.

After cutting the cove, you'll have to scrape and sand the profile to remove any machine marks. A gooseneck scraper comes in handy, but if you have a lot of molding to clean up, it's worth grinding a scraper to the exact shape of the cove. For the final sanding, make up a shaped sanding block, as shown in *Counterprofile Sanding Blocks*, on page 32.

ANGLED COVING

Once you get the hang of regular cove cutting, you can experiment with tilting the blade to create unusual profiles.

Tilting the blade when cove cutting can produce the undercut profile featured on this wooden drawer pull.

STEP BY STEP: COVE CUTTING ON THE TABLE SAW

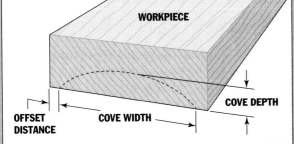

WORKPIECE

COVE DEPTH

OFFSET DISTANCE

COVE WIDTH

STEP 1 Lay out the cove on the end of the stock to determine its size and placement. Don't be too fussy, a sketch will do. Set your parallel rule so the space between the sticks equals the cove width.

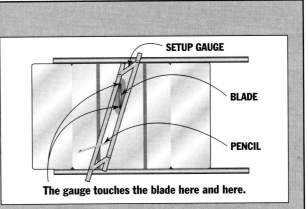

SETUP GAUGE

BLADE

PENCIL

The gauge touches the blade here and here.

STEP 2 Set the blade height to equal the cove depth. Straddle the blade with the gauge angling the blade to contact the blade as shown. Draw a line along the inner edge of the front stick.

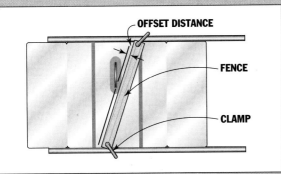

OFFSET DISTANCE

FENCE

CLAMP

STEP 3 Clamp an auxiliary fence to the saw table. The fence should be parallel to the pencil line but set away from the line by the offset distance you laid out on your workpiece.

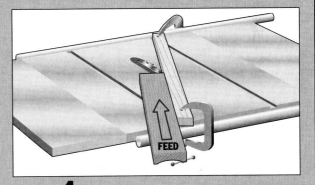

FEED

STEP 4 Set the blade to a height of about ¹⁄₁₆ inch. Guide the workpiece along the fence to make the first cut. Raise the blade ¹⁄₁₆ inch at a time until the cove is as deep as you want it.

RIPPINGS

CUTTING HALF A COVE

A cove cut makes a nice way to raise a panel for a door or a box lid without using a special bit. To cut a cove along the edge of a piece, angle an auxiliary fence as you would for a regular cove cut, but position the fence so it covers the front part of the blade, exposing only half the cutting arc. (You'll have to cut away a portion of the fence to provide clearance for the cutter.) Then shape the edge in light passes. Bullnose cutters in a molding head give the cleanest results, but a regular saw blade will work.

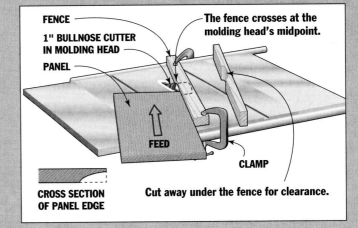

FENCE

1" BULLNOSE CUTTER IN MOLDING HEAD

PANEL

The fence crosses at the molding head's midpoint.

FEED

CLAMP

CROSS SECTION OF PANEL EDGE

Cut away under the fence for clearance.

Making Dowels

After plain old flat, the most common shaped surface probably is cylindrical, that is, a dowel. It's round in cross-section and straight in length. You can always buy dowel rods in diameters smaller than 1 inch, but what if you want a larger dowel, an odd size, or one made from a special hardwood? You'll have to make it. There are several ways to proceed.

Planing a Dowel

The photo at right shows an old dowel-making plane and two new ones. Would it surprise you to hear that the old one works better than the new ones? In fact, I have to confess that I can't make the new ones work at all. I think they should have been made from a thicker piece of wood with a longer bore.

You need a separate plane for each diameter of dowel you want to make. Set the blade to just kiss the surface of the finished dowel. You can see a paper shim tucked under the blade in the photo—it needed just that amount of lift to cut nicely.

Start with a square stick about $1/32$ inch larger than the diameter of the dowel you want. Chamfer the corner. You can go so far as to make the blank octagonal in sections, but you don't have to do more than knock off the corners. Hold the stock vertically in the vise, and twist the plane around it until the blade starts to cut. Once started, the plane works like an old-fashioned pencil sharpener.

If the dowel catches and the plane won't turn, the blade isn't set right. Its heel should just graze the finished diameter. If the dowel sticks and makes the plane difficult to turn, try waxing the bore of the plane with a little paraffin or paste wax.

Making Large Dowels

When you're making a large-diameter dowel like a curtain rod or a handrail, wood of the right

Dowel-making planes, sometimes called witchits, have a conical bore and a very sharp iron. You can make coarse adjustments to the blade by sliding it in or out. Make fine adjustments by adding shims behind the blade.

color is often more important than perfect roundness. You can make a pretty good dowel with a round-over bit of the approximate size in a table-mounted router. The sequence is shown in "Quick Dowels."

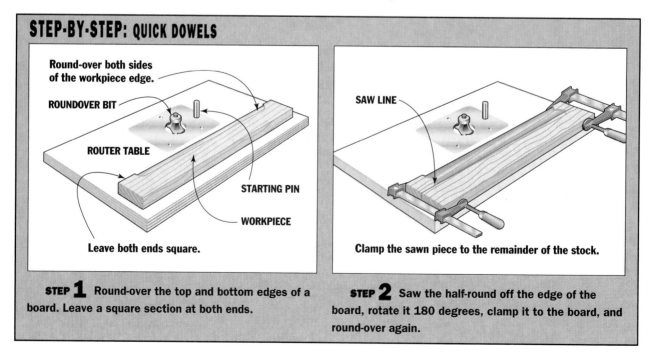

STEP-BY-STEP: QUICK DOWELS

Round-over both sides of the workpiece edge.

ROUNDOVER BIT

ROUTER TABLE

STARTING PIN

WORKPIECE

Leave both ends square.

SAW LINE

Clamp the sawn piece to the remainder of the stock.

STEP 1 Round-over the top and bottom edges of a board. Leave a square section at both ends.

STEP 2 Saw the half-round off the edge of the board, rotate it 180 degrees, clamp it to the board, and round-over again.

PUSHING THE LIMITS: Routing Dowels

You can make any size dowel you want with a router-and-drill jig. The jig guides a square stick of wood past a straight router bit. The drill rotates the stick, which goes in square and comes out round. You'll need a specific jig for each size dowel, although you can drill two different-sized dowel holes through the same jig block if you want, one on either side of the bit.

As shown in *A Dowel-Making Jig,* the jig body is a block of wood clamped onto the base of a router. Clamping the jig in place allows you to shift the jig slightly for adjustment.

Locate the center of the bit hole with a vee bit chucked in the router, while the block is clamped to the router base—no need to turn the power on. Unbolt the

block and drill the bit hole through the center of the block. To use a ½-inch straight bit, drill a ⅝-inch hole.

The hole for the dowel starts out the size of the square blank, measured corner to corner, and ends up the diameter of the finished dowel. It doesn't have to taper. It can simply be drilled with two sizes of bit—the large entrance hole first, half-way through the blank, then the small exit hole the rest of the way. The small hole should intersect the bit hole by ¹⁄₁₆ inch, so it will be tangent to the cutter itself. The transition from entry diameter to exit diameter occurs exactly at the center of the bit, as shown in the drawing.

Make the square blank ¹⁄₃₂ inch to ¹⁄₁₆ inch larger than the finished

dowel—less for small dowels, more for larger ones.

To use the jig, clamp it onto the router base, and hold the router upright in a bench vise, as shown in the photo below. You can't use the router table because you wouldn't have room for the drill that spins the stick.

Run the drill at medium speed, and feed steadily into the router cutter. Try spinning in both directions to see which produces the better cut. You'll have to fiddle a bit to get the jig positioned perfectly on the router. If the dowel comes out smaller than the exit hole, it will chatter and chip. If it is too big, it will bind in the jig, and the drill may twist the blank and break it. Be sure to make some extra blanks so you can waste a few getting the jig set up perfectly.

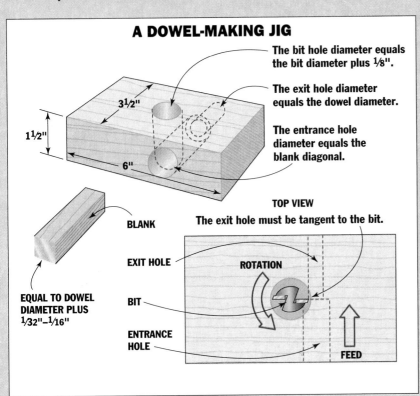

A DOWEL-MAKING JIG

3½"

1½"

6"

The bit hole diameter equals the bit diameter plus ⅛".

The exit hole diameter equals the dowel diameter.

The entrance hole diameter equals the blank diagonal.

BLANK

EXIT HOLE

BIT

ENTRANCE HOLE

EQUAL TO DOWEL DIAMETER PLUS ¹⁄₃₂"–¹⁄₁₆"

TOP VIEW
The exit hole must be tangent to the bit.

ROTATION

FEED

Drive the blanks through the dowel maker with an electric drill. Chuck small sticks directly in the drill. For larger sticks, try a suitable socket from a wrench set, plugged onto an extension, that fits the drill chuck. A square stick fits perfectly into a regular 12-point socket.

Tapering

A taper is a simple shape. It consists of two flat surfaces that aren't parallel to each other. You can cut tapers using the same shop tools that make parallel flat surfaces—table saw, band saw, jointer, thickness planer. The general method is to jig the workpiece so it is not parallel to the guiding fence or table, leaving the tool in its normal square position. Always cut and fit joints before cutting tapers, while the stock is still square.

Sawing Tapers

The table saw and the band saw both can cut excellent tapers using either of the two jigs shown in *Tapering Jigs*. For pieces that taper on one or two adjacent sides, the single-taper jig is all that is required. For pieces that taper on opposite sides or on all four sides, the double-taper jig is necessary. Once you cut the first side, you'll need to double the thickness of the stop block to cut the opposite side since you will have cut away that

You need a double-taper jig to taper all four sides of a leg. Cut two adjacent sides with the workpiece on the first step, then switch to the second step for the final two cuts.

much of the blank. This may sound confusing, but it will make perfect sense once you've tried it.

In general, I'd rather taper on the band saw because it's safer. On the band saw, you can feed either end of the workpiece into the blade first. I usually feed with the stop to the rear

because it helps push the workpiece through the cut. If you feed the other way, press on the workpiece to keep it in contact with the jig. Set the fence to the correct width and guide the jig along it to make the cut, as shown in the photo.

On the table saw, always feed with the stop end of the jig first, and push the workpiece, not the jig body. If you feed the other end first, the workpiece can get ahead of the jig, risking kickback. If I have more than four pieces to taper, I usually improve the jig by screwing it onto a plywood base that carries both the jig and the workpiece through the saw.

Jointing a Taper

It's easy enough to make an inadvertent taper on the jointer, so it's no wonder this machine does such an excellent job when that's your goal. The setup is nothing more than a stop block clamped to the infeed table, as shown in *Tapering on the Jointer*. Start out with the jointer set to take a cut about $1/8$ inch deep.

The precise amount of taper depends on depth of cut plus the

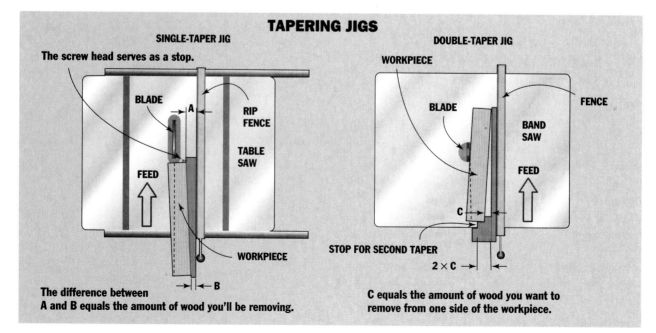

TAPERING JIGS

SINGLE-TAPER JIG

The screw head serves as a stop.

BLADE

A

RIP FENCE

TABLE SAW

FEED

WORKPIECE

B

The difference between A and B equals the amount of wood you'll be removing.

DOUBLE-TAPER JIG

WORKPIECE

BLADE

FENCE

BAND SAW

FEED

C

STOP FOR SECOND TAPER

$2 \times C$

C equals the amount of wood you want to remove from one side of the workpiece.

location of the stop block and the number of passes you take. You could experiment to get it figured out so you can get the taper you want with an exact number of passes. But it's probably quicker to fudge the process a little by making lighter and shorter cuts once you get close to the layout line. A final, full-length clean-up cut will remove the bumps.

As a variation of jointer tapering, you can create a spade-foot detail on the end of a table leg. Taper the leg first, so the foot doesn't look too clunky, then clamp a stop block to the outfeed table, as shown in *Jointing a Spade Foot*. To make the foot, hold the workpiece against the infeed stop block and lower the piece into the cut. Feed it forward until it reaches the outfeed stop block, then lift it carefully. Rotate the workpiece to cut the other sides. Then, lower the infeed table about $\frac{1}{8}$ inch, and make another pass on each side. Continue until the foot is as bold as you want it. Don't make a really heavy cut, or you may blow the foot off the end of the leg.

Planing a Taper

By building a jig to hold the workpiece on an incline, you can taper wide pieces with a thickness planer. The jig is simply a ramp mounted on a baseplate with a stop block at both ends, as shown in *Tapering with a Planer*. The slope of the ramp equals the slope of the taper. Set the workpiece against the stop block, and feed the whole assembly through the planer, with the low end of the ramp entering first. For safety, extend the baseplate 9 inches to 12 inches beyond the ramp at both ends.

You'll have to hand propel the jig for the first pass or two. This creates an initial flat for the feed rollers to grip. Push or pull on the extended baseplate, and be sure your hands **never** enter the portal of the machine. Once you've established a flat, the feed rollers will grab and feed the fixture and workpiece together, just as if they were a normal board.

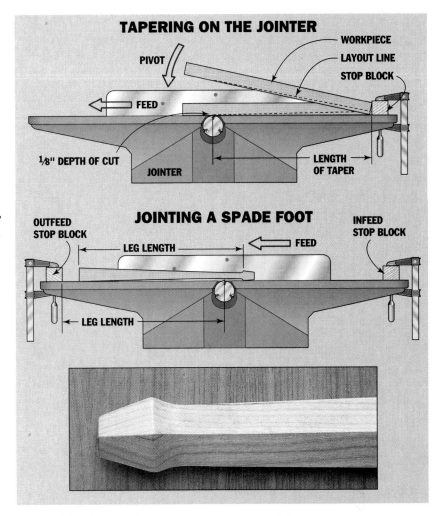

TAPERING ON THE JOINTER

PIVOT • WORKPIECE • LAYOUT LINE • STOP BLOCK • FEED • $\frac{1}{8}$" DEPTH OF CUT • JOINTER • LENGTH OF TAPER

JOINTING A SPADE FOOT

OUTFEED STOP BLOCK • LEG LENGTH • FEED • INFEED STOP BLOCK • LEG LENGTH

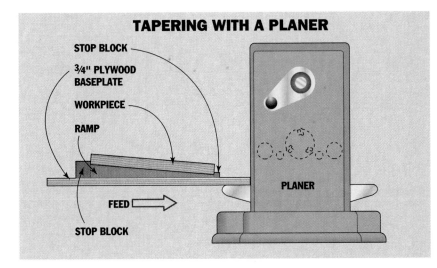

TAPERING WITH A PLANER

STOP BLOCK • $\frac{3}{4}$" PLYWOOD BASEPLATE • WORKPIECE • RAMP • FEED • STOP BLOCK • PLANER

Making Shapely Legs

Shaped legs often determine the style of a piece of furniture. The cabriole leg of the Queen Anne era is a popular style, but the same techniques can make other shapes, too. Legs always come in multiples of twos and fours—there's never just one to make, so it makes sense to develop patterns for efficiency.

The cabriole shape develops from a single pattern, which you trace onto two adjacent faces of the wood, as shown in the photo. The problem is, when you saw one face of the wood, you also saw the layout off the adjacent face. The most common way of dealing with this problem involves tape and luck—you tape the cutoff back in place and hope it stays there while you saw the second side. My method keeps the layout intact on both faces, leaving tape

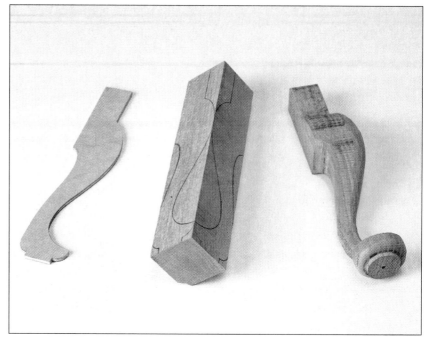

The three-dimensional cabriole leg is laid out with the help of a two-dimensional pattern. The profiles are sawn on the band saw.

as your fall-back position if things don't quite work out.

Cutting the Leg

Begin by developing a full-sized leg pattern from your working drawing. From the pattern, you can figure the dimensions of the wooden blanks you need. Try to leave ⅛ inch of clearance between the knee and the edge of the wood. This extra gives you some

---

STEP-BY-STEP: CUTTING A CABRIOLE LEG

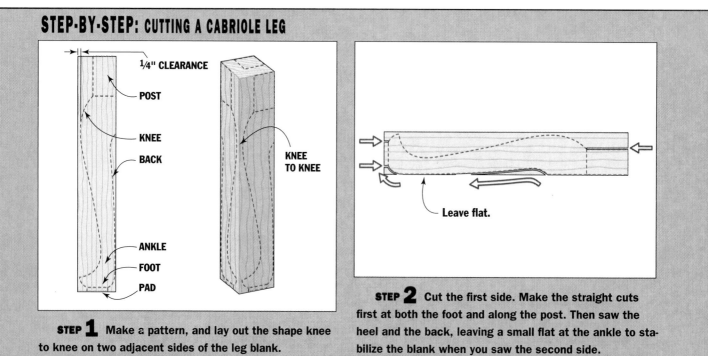

¼" CLEARANCE
POST
KNEE
BACK
KNEE TO KNEE
ANKLE
FOOT
PAD

Leave flat.

STEP 1 Make a pattern, and lay out the shape knee to knee on two adjacent sides of the leg blank.

STEP 2 Cut the first side. Make the straight cuts first at both the foot and along the post. Then saw the heel and the back, leaving a small flat at the ankle to stabilize the blank when you saw the second side.

leeway in sawing. Prepare all of the blanks, and trace the pattern onto two adjacent faces of each blank, as shown in **STEP 1** of "Cutting a Cabriole Leg." Make sure you orient the two layouts knee to knee, not back to back. Laying out this way puts the flatter surfaces of the leg down on the saw table, stabilizing the blank.

Before you saw the leg, lay out and cut the mortises in the post section. It's always easier to make mortises while the workpiece is square. To saw the leg, equip the band saw with a ¼-inch 4 tpi (teeth per inch) or 6 tpi blade. Cut one side, then the other, as explained in **STEP 2**, **STEP 3**, and **STEP 4** of "Cutting a Cabriole Leg."

Finishing the Leg

The easiest way to complete the leg is with a pneumatic drum sander. It will smooth off all the corners quickly and help you blend the various facets to create a pleasing contour. If you don't

have a drum sander, you can always default to spokeshaves, Surforms, files, and sandpaper.

Draw guidelines on the sawn leg to locate the finished surface you want. Knock off the corners and remove all of the band-saw marks before you begin to fuss with the detailed shapes. Make

the ankle a neat circle or oval in cross section, and flow the knee and foot into it. Complete one leg so that you can be sure about where you are going before you dig into the rest of them.

Note: the pad on the bottom of a cabriole leg is often turned on a lathe to hasten the process.

TROUBLESHOOTING

SHAPING LEGS

A spokeshave is the traditional tool for refining the curves of a cabriole leg. A flat-bottomed shave does the convex parts of the form, and a round-bottomed one does the concavities. However, spokeshaves aren't easy tools to use. If the tool chatters and skips, it's set for too coarse a cut, so you need to back the blade up. If you can't get the blade to bite, even though it's sharp, try easing up on your grip. The spokeshave will find its own angle relative to the surface of the wood, if you let it. Grasp the handles as loosely as you can, and pull the cutting edge toward you. Let one handle lead the other, so the blade is at an angle to the line of travel.

The Stanley Surform is a good alternative to the spokeshave. The replaceable blades look like cheese graters. To get anywhere on a curved surface, you need two Surforms: a flat one and a round one. You'll get best results if you pay close attention to grain direction, the same as with any other cutting tool.

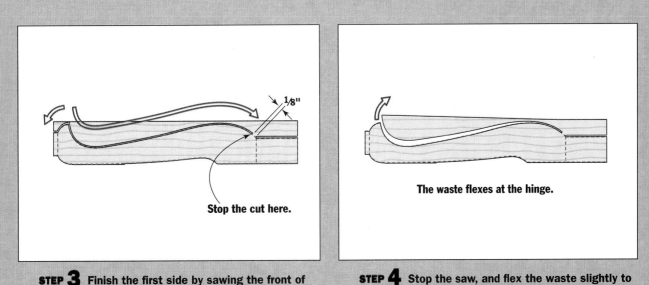

STEP 3 Finish the first side by sawing the front of the foot. Also saw the front of the leg and around the knee. Stop the cut ⅛ inch from the post, leaving a hinge of wood.

STEP 4 Stop the saw, and flex the waste slightly to back the blade out of the cut. Repeat the sequence on the adjacent face. This way the layout should be intact except for a little bit at the foot that you can pencil in.

Shaping a Chair Seat

A chair seat combines concave and convex curves in one fully sculpted form. My method for shaping a batch of chair seats uses a pattern with an electric drill to establish the depth of the hollow at regular points across the surface, as shown in "Pattern-Carving Chair Seats." Once I've drilled these points, I remove the waste with power-carving tools. This method is very good for making more than one chair seat.

Carving the Pattern

Chair-Seat Pattern shows the basic contour for a Windsor-style seat. Make a saddle gauge, which shows the contour along the center of the seat, to guide the work. Develop your own full-size paper pattern and gauge from published drawings or from a chair you like. A seat hollow is not actually very deep: $5/8$ inch to $3/4$ inch at the most. Draw contour lines on the pattern to show various depths.

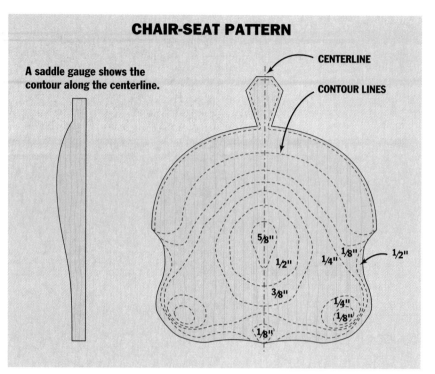

CHAIR-SEAT PATTERN

A saddle gauge shows the contour along the centerline.

CENTERLINE

CONTOUR LINES

Most chair seats are carved from 2-inch thick wood with the grain running from front to back. Since most chairs are wider at the front than at the back, orienting the grain this way keeps the legs from penetrating the seat along the same grain lines, which might cause the seat to split. Make your pattern from an easy-to-work wood like pine or poplar, and prepare it for hollowing by cutting the outside contour on the band saw.

Two tools, the carbide burr and the chain-saw-tooth–carving disk, have recently been invented for power carving as shown in the photos at left. Burrs can be chucked in an electric drill, in a die grinder, or in the hand piece of a flexible-shaft tool such as a Dremel. They come in different grits and sizes. They'll work across the grain as well as with it.

The chain-saw-tooth–carving disk removes wood much faster than the burr, but it is more dangerous. It's also easy to carve too far. Until you get the knack, the teeth may grab the wood and skitter across it. It throws a lot of high-velocity debris, so you need to wear gloves and a face shield.

If you do a lot of contouring, your best approach may be to rough out the shape with the carving disk, then refine the shape with the burr.

Start carving at the deepest portion of the seat, but don't go directly to full depth. Work back and forth

A chain-saw-tooth–carving disk (left) must be mounted on a right-angle grinder, not on an electric drill, because the grinder has a built-in guard. A carbide-burr (right) isn't as quick, but it's a lot easier to use and control.

Problem Solving
Sculpting Chair Seats

Carving a chair seat isn't easy. Even when using a pattern, it is still possible to carve too far.
There are ways to recover from a slip of the gouge, however.

PROBLEM	SOLUTION
I carved my chair seat pattern too deep in one area.	With a pattern, carving too deep isn't much of a problem. Bring the area up to level with auto-body compound.
I slipped and carved one of my actual chair seats too deep. Do I have to scrap the entire piece?	Not necessarily. While a filler won't look good, you may be able to rip the seat on the band saw, cutting away the gouged area. Then glue in a new piece of wood and carve it level with the surrounding area.

across the seat, extending the hollow toward the edges as you make it deeper. As you approach full depth, blend any stair steps into one another in order to create a fair curve from front to back and side to side. Check the contours with your seat gauge, with your eye, and with your hand.

Smoothing the Pattern

Once you've established the basic form of the seat blank, remove the scars caused by the roughing-down tools. You can use carving gouges, but I prefer a coarse sanding disk—24 grit or so—stuck on a soft rubber pad and mounted in a right-angle grinder. The grinder is much more effective than a drill-mounted sanding disk because it gives you a working handle right where you need it.

Keep the disk moving back and forth across the surface of the wood, so its edge doesn't dig in. Don't worry about scratches until after you've created a uniform surface.

If you're making a pattern in order to carve more seats, quit sanding once you've established the basic contour. If you are making a finished seat, continue to smooth the wood until you're completely satisfied with it. You'll be able to remove most of the sanding swirls with increasingly fine disks, but the final sanding will have to be done by hand.

Pattern-Carving Seats

To carve a batch of seats, drill through the pattern to lay out the blanks. Once the contour is transferred, you can start carving. When you carve each seat, connect the holes in dot-to-dot fashion. When you've just removed the dimple at the bottom of each hole, you will have reproduced the contour of the pattern.

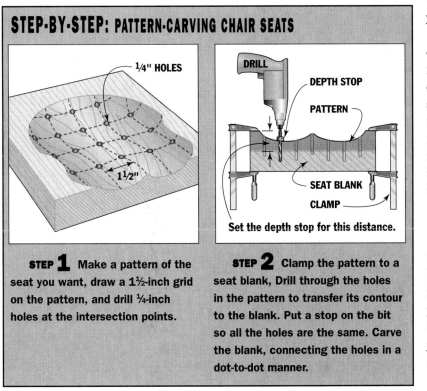

STEP-BY-STEP: PATTERN-CARVING CHAIR SEATS

STEP 1 Make a pattern of the seat you want, draw a 1½-inch grid on the pattern, and drill ¼-inch holes at the intersection points.

STEP 2 Clamp the pattern to a seat blank, Drill through the holes in the pattern to transfer its contour to the blank. Put a stop on the bit so all the holes are the same. Carve the blank, connecting the holes in a dot-to-dot manner.

Carving a Bowl

Unseasoned wood is the secret of the traditional dough bowl and other deep woodenware. If your woodworking has been confined to seasoned wood, for a completely different experience, you really ought to try working with green, fresh-cut logs. You may be able to get some from your local tree surgeon.

The secret of the traditional dough bowl is to carve it from green wood. This is a real antidote to the fussiness of conventional woodworking.

Wet wood is relatively easy to split, carve, and shape with sharp edge tools. However, it will shrink and deform while drying, which is why you can't use it for furniture and cabinetwork. Distortion and shrinkage won't affect the loose form of a bowl or a trough, provided you allow the wood to dry slowly so it doesn't check and crack.

You can see the shape of a bowl in a half-log of wood, and for your first time out, it's best to work with this shape. You can use almost any close-grained wood. Hardwoods like walnut and cherry are relatively easy to work green, and woods like white pine and tulip poplar are a dream. Choose a straight-grained, knot-free log, crosscut it to eliminate checks or splits, and split it in half to create your blank.

Carvers differ on which to shape first, the outside or the inside. I prefer to start with the outside, then to hollow the inside to match. It's easier to keep track of the wall thickness this way. And if there is a fatal defect in the wood, you'll find it before you put any time into hollowing.

Hewing the Outside

Stand the blank on a chopping block, and hew the outside with a small hatchet, as shown in the photo above right. Establish a rhythm with the tool as you work first one end of the blank, then the other. Don't worry about details, just rough out the shape, then go immediately to the inside. If you have to leave the work for more

Rough out the outside of the bowl with a hatchet. Cut with the grain, from the bottom gradually working the ends to shape to the lip.

than a few minutes, bury it under its own chips, or stick it in a plastic bag so the freshly cut wood doesn't lose surface moisture and begin to check.

Hollowing the Inside

Now stand the bowl upright to hollow out the inside, as shown in the photo below. Your biggest problem will be persuading it to hold

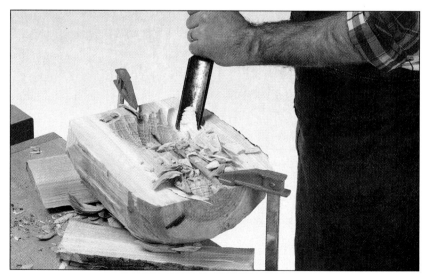

Work the inside of the bowl on your bench with stout carving gouges. Use wedges and clamps to hold the bowl in place.

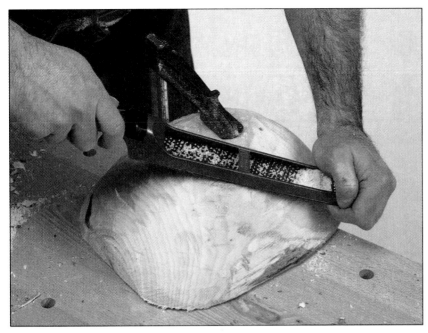

Smooth the hatchet marks off the outside with a Surform rasp.

Carving gouges are about the only choice you have for finishing off the inside of a deep bowl. You need a wide, bent gouge with a No. 2 or No. 3 shallow sweep. You'll achieve a nicer surface if you push the gouge by hand, instead of with the mallet. The most difficult place to finish is the inside bottom. All your cuts have to come out even here, and you have to work across the grain, as shown in the photo below, in order to avoid digging a trench.

Let the bowl sit for a couple of days before you complete it. If the weather is dry, cover it so it dries more slowly. The wood is certain to twist and move, but it probably won't crack. Carve over the whole thing again, inside and out, to pare off any remaining hills and valleys. A small Surform with a curved sole may help on the inside. Finally, sand the entire bowl with 80-grit and 120-grit sandpaper.

still. I like to work standing at the bench, so I usually stick a wedge under one edge of the bowl and clamp that side to the bench top, while I work on the other edge. Use a fairly deep gouge, a No. 5 or No. 7 sweep that's 1 inch or more wide. Work your way out from the center toward the rim of the bowl, driving your gouge into the wood with a wooden mallet. Excavate the whole cavity to about the same depth, then if you need to go deeper, excavate the whole area to the next depth. To make sure you don't go too far, check the depth with your fingers and with a ruler in the deeper parts of the bowl. You'll need a bent gouge or a spoon gouge to shape the bottom of the cavity, a chairmaker's scorp can be a help, too.

Stand back and take a good look at the shape you're making. If it's lopsided, rough it into line. Try to complete the general adjustment of the shape with roughing tools, before you start to refine the surfaces. You can clean up the outside

of the bowl with carving tools, a drawknife, and a spokeshave, but I prefer a Surform rasp, as shown in the photo above. The Surform works quickly, and it seems to like the leathery texture of wood that has started to dry out.

It's difficult to smooth the bottom of the bowl because the grain changes direction there. Take shallow cuts with a sharp gouge. Working across the grain gives the best results.

6
OTHER SHAPING TOOLS

Key Ingredients

Just as the piano may be considered the principal instrument of music, so the router is the principal shaping tool in the small woodworking shop. With a good router and router table, plus some ingenuity and patience, you can turn a pile of rough boards into a piece of furniture.

However, just as you can't play a violin sonata with a piano, the router is not the best tool for every shaping task. To work efficiently in a wood shop, especially when it comes to cutting shapes and profiles, you'll want to take advantage of the specialized strengths of other shop tools. Here are three from the top of my list:

- The table-saw molding head is a close cousin to the kind of tooling that's used on industrial shapers, and it converts your table saw into a shaper of sorts. As shown in the photo above right, a molding head is a heavy metal plate with three slots cut into its rim. An Allen screw securely locks a high-speed steel cutter into each of the slots. The manufacturers who make molding heads sell a reasonable variety of cutter shapes. However, their systems for locking the cutters into the

A table-saw molding head and a set of cutters like these give you great flexibility for shaping. You can even cut shapes in the face of a wide board where a router can't reach.

head vary, so the cutters are not interchangeable from manufacturer to manufacturer.

The advantage of the table-saw molding head over the router table is that the workpiece can lie flat on the saw table. This means you can easily cut shapes like flutes and beads into the face of a wide board. The same operation on the router table or shaper has to be done with the stock up on edge, and how high above the

table you can raise the bit or cutter limits the location of the cut on the face of a board.

- The lathe spins the workpiece against a stationary cutter, instead of the other way around. You can start out with straight and square stock and make spindles for table legs, balusters, and the like. Or you can make bowls. The lathe can make such specific shapes as corner blocks, or rosettes—flat, circular ornaments for furniture and millwork. You can also make larger circular frames; see *Shaping with a Lathe*.

The lathe can also be used in combination with a router. When you mount your router on top of a lathe, as shown in "Box Jig for Routing Flutes and Reeds" on page 85, you can rout shapes along the length of a turned cylinder. This is the way to make things like fluted columns or reeded table pedestals.

● The shaper is the grandpa of today's router, and this book would be incomplete without some discussion of this machine. It does many of the same things a router does and some things a router can't do, but it doesn't operate on any different principle. Just like a router, the shaper is a motor-driven spindle with cutters mounted on it.

There are two big differences between a shaper and a table-mounted router. The first is heft: A shaper typically has a cast-iron table, a heavier and more powerful motor, and a thicker spindle as shown in the photo at right. The second is speed. Shapers operate between 5,000 rpm and 10,000 rpm, whereas a router ramps up to 22,000 rpm. Consequently, a shaper can swing a much larger cutter than a router, and it can remove more stock at one time. You could shape a handrail, for example, with a single cutter on the shaper, while the same profile would require a number of different router bits. Other processes, like raising panels and making cope-and-stick frames, can be done far more efficiently on the shaper.

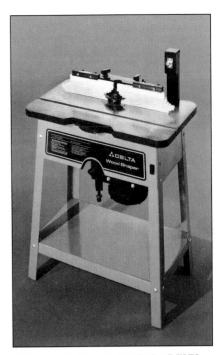

This small shaper, made by DELTA, has a cast-iron table with a cross-cut slot, a split fence, ¾-inch spindle, and 2-horsepower motor. Many manufacturers make a similar model for the small shop.

Does this mean you should rush out and replace your router table? Probably not. Industrial shapers are big, heavy machines, designed for all-day operation. Their cutters are also big and heavy—and expensive. You can get a light-duty shaper, but the lighter it is, the less it will perform like a shaper and the more it will perform like the router table you already have.

A few other tools for shaping wood are mentioned briefly in this chapter: the planer/molder (page 81), the drill press (page 83), and the pin router (page 87). These machines do have some special uses worth knowing about, but they are either limited in what they can do as shaping tools or so expensive that they are hard to justify having in a small home shop.

SHAPING WITH A LATHE

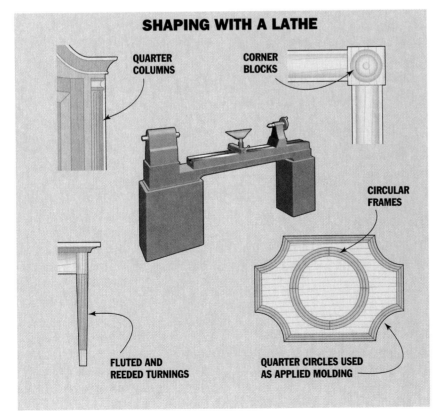

QUARTER COLUMNS

CORNER BLOCKS

CIRCULAR FRAMES

FLUTED AND REEDED TURNINGS

QUARTER CIRCLES USED AS APPLIED MOLDING

Shaping with a Table-Saw Molding Head

The table-saw molding head is an excellent alternative to the router and the shaper. With this tool, you can cut multiple flutes and coves to form pilasters and door casings, as shown in the photo at right—something that's difficult to accomplish with a router or shaper. The molding head comes with a thick spacer, which mounts on the saw arbor first. The spacer moves the head away from the saw's innards, which it otherwise might hit.

You must buy or make a special table insert for the molding head. A standard metal dado insert is too narrow. Whereas you can cut the slot in a wooden dado insert by raising the cutters into it, you shouldn't try the same maneuver with a molding head. The molding-head cutters are liable to jam and kick back the insert. Instead, lay out the slot in a piece of plywood, and rout it.

In many applications, panel raising, for example, you'll be

Cutting profiles into the face of a wide board is where the molding head excels. The table-saw fence makes the setup quick and accurate.

working with the stock up on edge. The standard table-saw rip fence is too narrow to support a wide workpiece. Make a high auxiliary fence by screwing a piece of plywood onto the regular rip fence.

In some cases, you'll be able to make the same profile with the workpiece up on edge or flat on the table. Whenever possible, I prefer to work flat on the table because it's safer. When you are working up on edge, be sure you don't trap the workpiece between the cutter and the fence. Add an auxiliary wood fence to enclose the cutter with the working portion projecting from it; see **STEPS 3** and **4** in "Shaping a Chair Rail with a Table-Saw Molding Head."

As with all shaping operations, smooth and accurate stock feeding is essential. If the wood doesn't lie

---

RIPPINGS

HONING MOLDING-HEAD CUTTERS

New molding-head cutters will have been finished on a surface grinding wheel, which raises a burr that the manufacturing process does not bother to remove. You can improve new cutters significantly by honing their flat sides on a diamond lap or on a fine bench stone to remove the burr, as shown in the photo below. You might have to knock a burr off the cutting bevel as well, but you shouldn't try to sharpen the bevel. If you sharpen the cutters unequally, the edge profile will vary from one to the other. Then only one or two of the cutters will be cutting the wood, which will result in a rougher surface. If your cutters need regrinding, send them to a professional sharpening service.

Knock the burr off the edge of a molding-head cutter by rubbing the flat back on a sharpening stone. Hone all three cutters equally. Don't try to sharpen the bevel or you will end up with three slightly different profiles.

flat on the saw table and tight against the fence, the profile will be rippled and not uniform.

Here are some things to bear in mind when using a molding head:

- Never run a three-knife cutter head with only one or two knives in place, or it will be dangerously off balance.
- To make narrow moldings, always mill the profile in the edges of a wider board, then rip to finished width. One of the disadvantages of the molding head is you'll have to tear down the setup in order to rip to width, then change back to the molding head in order to run more material.
- The molding head exerts considerable upward pressure on the workpiece. You'll get best results by making multiple passes, raising the cutter after each pass, and feeding slowly. Support rollers, fingerboards, and other hold-downs will all improve the quality of the cut.
- Don't use molding-head cutters on plywood. The steel knives will dull in no time.
- When you combine molding knives to make multiple cuts, your results aren't likely to be as neat as the ones shown in the owner's manual. Plane or sand the pieces to blend the shapes into one another.

Making Moldings

You can create a variety of molding profiles with the table-saw molding head by cutting a series of separate shapes into the stock. The chair rail shown in "Shaping a Chair Rail with a Table-Saw Molding Head" is a good example. It can be made with a 1-inch cove cutter and a ¼-inch beader. Here you're shaping the entire face of the stock, and the trick is planning the sequence of cuts so you always have flat stock bearing against the table or fence or both.

Note that in **STEPS 3** and **4**, the cutter is buried partly under an auxiliary wooden fence attached to the table-saw fence. Also, in **STEP 3**, the fence is on the left side of the cutter. This is often necessary in order to use the part of the cutter that you want. Finally, note that in **STEP 4**, you'll be cutting away part of the stock that's riding against the fence. The piece can tip a little at the very end of the cut. Set up a fingerboard raised off the table to keep pressure at the top of the stock where it's in contact with the fence.

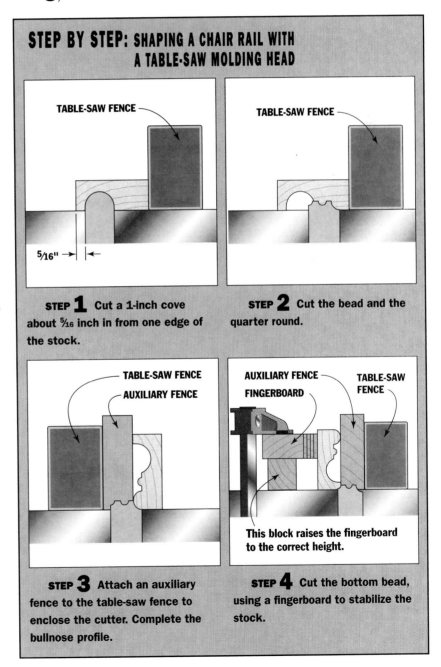

STEP BY STEP: SHAPING A CHAIR RAIL WITH A TABLE-SAW MOLDING HEAD

TABLE-SAW FENCE

5/16"

STEP 1 Cut a 1-inch cove about ⁵⁄₁₆ inch in from one edge of the stock.

TABLE-SAW FENCE

STEP 2 Cut the bead and the quarter round.

TABLE-SAW FENCE
AUXILIARY FENCE

STEP 3 Attach an auxiliary fence to the table-saw fence to enclose the cutter. Complete the bullnose profile.

AUXILIARY FENCE
FINGERBOARD
TABLE-SAW FENCE

This block raises the fingerboard to the correct height.

STEP 4 Cut the bottom bead, using a fingerboard to stabilize the stock.

Using a Molding Head on the Radial-Arm Saw

The table-saw molding head can also be used on most radial-arm saws. There is one important difference: The motor must be turned up vertical, so the cutterhead is parallel to the surface of the table. **Do not** use the molding head on a radial-arm saw with the motor in the standard position. This would trap the workpiece between the cutter and the table, and a kickback would be virtually certain. You will need to make an auxiliary fence with an opening large enough for the molding cutters to protrude. The radial-arm–saw/molding-head combination more nearly resembles a shaper than does the table-saw/molding-head setup.

There are two ways in which the radial-arm–saw setup is more versatile than the table-saw setup. First, you can shape the entire edge of the stock using a split fence. This would be identical to the split fence technique for the router table discussed in "Shaping the Whole Edge" on page 22, but adapted to the radial-arm saw.

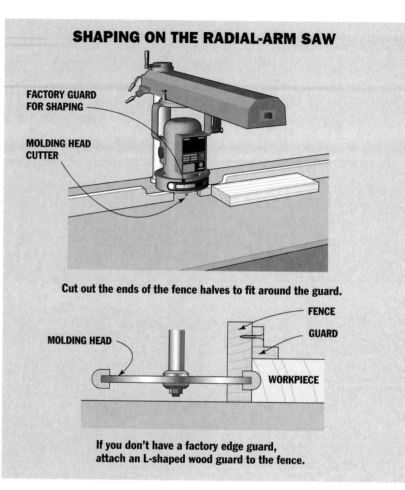

SHAPING ON THE RADIAL-ARM SAW

FACTORY GUARD FOR SHAPING

MOLDING HEAD CUTTER

Cut out the ends of the fence halves to fit around the guard.

FENCE

GUARD

MOLDING HEAD

WORKPIECE

If you don't have a factory edge guard, attach an L-shaped wood guard to the fence.

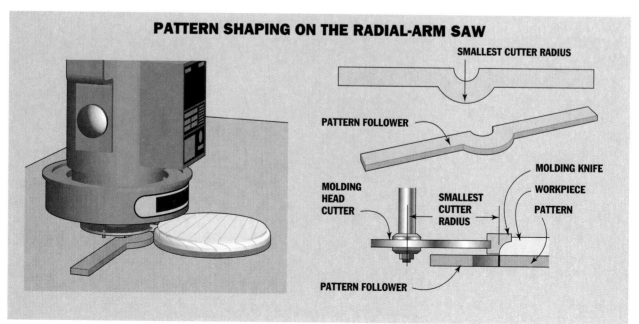

PATTERN SHAPING ON THE RADIAL-ARM SAW

SMALLEST CUTTER RADIUS

PATTERN FOLLOWER

MOLDING HEAD CUTTER

SMALLEST CUTTER RADIUS

MOLDING KNIFE

WORKPIECE

PATTERN

PATTERN FOLLOWER

PLANER-MOLDER

Industrial planer-molder machines often combine multiple operations, such as ripping, surface planing, face molding, and edge molding. These machines contain a separate cutterhead for each operation, and they can produce finished flooring, window and door parts, or completed moldings in one pass. Smaller planer-molders, like the one shown in the photo at left, do the same range of planing and shaping operations, but they have a single cutterhead into which you insert pairs of knives—shaped ones for molding and straight ones for planing. On some machines, you can keep the planer knives in the head permanently, and install molding cutters in the same head without removing the planer knives. This arrangement makes switching from one to the other much easier.

A big advantage of shaping with planer/molders is that they shape the face of the board with the wood lying flat on the table. Also, the smaller models are sized and priced within the reach of the small workshop. If you are planning to produce a house full of millwork, you should consider one of these machines.

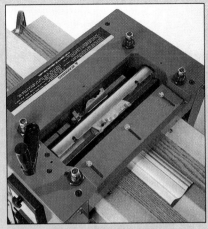

Small planer-molders combine a molding head with a surface planer. On this model, made by JET, some molding knives can be inserted without removing the planer blades.

Second, the orientation of the cutter permits you to shape the edge of a convex-curved workpiece. More on that later.

In other ways, the radial-arm setup is less versatile than the molding head on the table saw. The bulky motor and yoke may get in the way so you can't access the full profile of the cutter. And you can't orient the stock on edge because the motor gets in the way. Consequently, you can't cut a profile into the face of a wide board.

A guard for shaping on the radial-arm saw was at one time available as an accessory to the machine, but it's not available anymore. It's up to you to analyze the setup that you have, and make a wooden guard you can screw onto the fence or clamp onto the table, so you can't accidentally move your fingers near the cutterhead.

For shaping straight edges on the radial-arm saw, follow this sequence of steps:

STEP 1 Mount the cutters into the molding head, and then mount the molding head onto the radial-arm–saw shaft.

STEP 2 Rotate the saw motor 90 degrees, and then rotate the entire yoke assembly 90 degrees into the position for shaping, as shown in *Using a Molding Head on the Radial-Arm Saw*.

STEP 3 Slide the yoke back as far as it will go toward the column and lock it on the arm.

STEP 4 Adjust the height of the cutter by raising or lowering the radial-arm assembly.

STEP 5 Attach a two-piece fence to the table, and set the depth of cut.

STEP 6 If you don't have a factory-made shaper guard for your saw, make an L-shaped one, as shown in *Using A Molding Head on the Radial-Arm Saw* on page 80, and screw it onto the fence. The guard can rest right on the workpiece, acting like a hold-down at the same time.

You can also shape the edge of a convex curve on the radial-arm saw. To do this, you need to set up a pattern follower below the cutterhead. The pattern follower operates like a bearing on a router bit, and with it, you can duplicate parts from a plywood pattern attached to the workpiece, as shown in *Pattern Shaping on the Radial-Arm Saw*. Note that the radius of the pattern follower should equal the radius of the cutterhead at its smallest point. Attach the pattern follower to the straight fence or directly to the radial-arm–saw table in place of the fence. Take a series of light passes, especially on small workpieces, lowering the motor after each cut.

Turning Shapes and Profiles

Beyond making spindles and bowls, the lathe can make corner blocks, circular moldings and frames, and quarter columns. It also serves as an indexed work-holding fixture for reeding and fluting columns. If you are shopping for a lathe that you intend to use for this kind of work, make sure it has an indexing plate built into the head stock. An indexing plate is a metal disk with 24, 48, 60, 72, or 96 evenly spaced holes drilled around its circumference, allowing you to divide a turning into equal segments.

Turned Corner Blocks

Corner blocks, or rosettes, are a nice alternative to mitering the corners of molded casings around doors and windows, as shown in *Turned Corner Blocks*. The straight run of molding butts right into the corner block, so all the pieces can be cut square.

If you make the corner block about ⅛ inch thicker and ½ inch wider than the casing itself, the offset will conceal variations due to wood movement. Turned rosettes look good with plain casings. If you intend to use them with molded casings, don't make a lot of ditzy little beads and listels. Your eye won't separate them. Aim instead for broad bands of shadow and a nicely domed center button, concave or convex, as shown in *Turned Corner Blocks*.

Trimming out the doors and windows of a whole house will require a surprising number of corner blocks. This means you need a quick way of mounting the blank on the faceplate of the lathe.

You can make or buy a screw chuck for turning a corner block but you have to be careful not to hit the screw while turning. A better approach is to make a wedge-fit faceplate chuck. With this, you force-fit the corner block into a square opening, turn the profile, then pry out the finished block. Create the square opening by

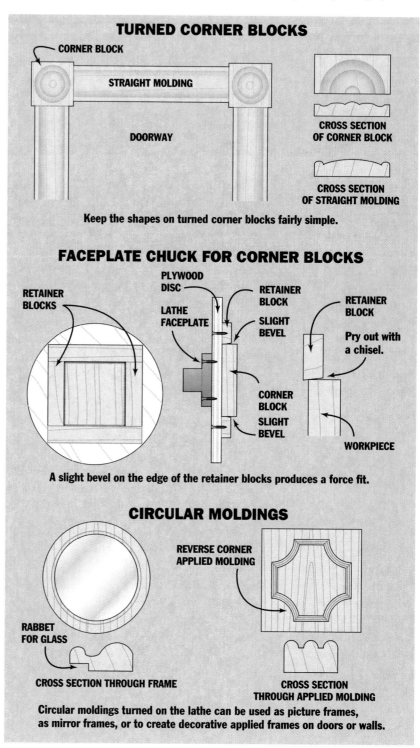

TURNED CORNER BLOCKS

CORNER BLOCK

STRAIGHT MOLDING

DOORWAY

CROSS SECTION OF CORNER BLOCK

CROSS SECTION OF STRAIGHT MOLDING

Keep the shapes on turned corner blocks fairly simple.

FACEPLATE CHUCK FOR CORNER BLOCKS

RETAINER BLOCKS

PLYWOOD DISC

LATHE FACEPLATE

RETAINER BLOCK

SLIGHT BEVEL

RETAINER BLOCK

Pry out with a chisel.

CORNER BLOCK

SLIGHT BEVEL

WORKPIECE

A slight bevel on the edge of the retainer blocks produces a force fit.

CIRCULAR MOLDINGS

REVERSE CORNER APPLIED MOLDING

RABBET FOR GLASS

CROSS SECTION THROUGH FRAME

CROSS SECTION THROUGH APPLIED MOLDING

Circular moldings turned on the lathe can be used as picture frames, as mirror frames, or to create decorative applied frames on doors or walls.

RIPPINGS

SHAPING ON THE DRILL PRESS

With a rosette cutter in the drill press, you can shape turned corner blocks or wheels for children's toys. The cutter shown in the photo drills a center hole, while other designs do not. Always clamp the workpiece to the drill-press table because otherwise these cutters may grab and spin the work. The drill press is not capable of heavy shaping work because the spindle speed is too slow and the bearings are not designed for side loads.

The rosette cutter can make small "turnings," like corner blocks for door casings and wheels for toys.

STEP BY STEP: TURNING A CIRCULAR FRAME

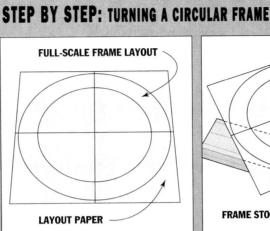

FULL-SCALE FRAME LAYOUT

LAYOUT PAPER

STEP 1 Draw the circular frame full size on a piece of paper, and divide it into quadrants.

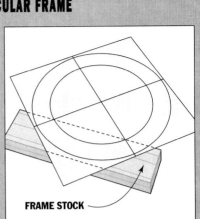

FRAME STOCK

STEP 2 Lay out the length and width of the stock needed for each quadrant of the circle.

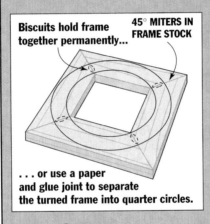

Biscuits hold frame together permanently...

45° MITERS IN FRAME STOCK

... or use a paper and glue joint to separate the turned frame into quarter circles.

STEP 3 Miter the ends of the stock at 45 degrees. Cut biscuit joints, then glue up the frame. Make sure the biscuits fall within the part of the frame you intend to keep.

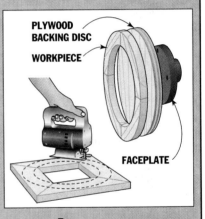

PLYWOOD BACKING DISC

WORKPIECE

FACEPLATE

STEP 4 Cut the inside and outside of the circle with a saber saw, then attach the frame to a plywood faceplate. True up the edges first, then turn the profile on the face.

---

attaching retainer blocks to a wooden face plate, as shown in *Faceplate Chuck for Corner Blocks*. To create the wedge effect, plane about a 1-degree bevel on the inside edges of the retainer blocks. Tap each block into the chuck. If the fit is too loose, add paper shims. When you're done turning, lever the block out of the chuck with a bench chisel.

Making Circular Moldings

You can turn a circular molding or a quarter-circle corner to match a straight molding. *Circular Moldings* shows two ways to use these turnings.

Most circular moldings are pieced together as shown in "Turning a Circular Frame." If you plan to use the molding in quarters, make a paper and glue joint so you

can separate the quadrants cleanly after turning.

If you want a rabbet for glass, make it in **STEP 4** before turning the face profile. Attach the frame to the plywood faceplate with double-faced carpet tape, and turn the rabbet into the back side of the disk first. Then reverse the ring to turn the face profile. You could also rout the rabbet with a bearing-guided rabbetting bit after the frame is turned.

Fluting and Reeding Columns

You can shape flutes and reeds into flat stock with a router or table-saw molding head. But with a lathe and a scratch stock or a router, you can mold flutes and reeds in turned columns. The technique is straight-forward: Turn a smooth column, then use the lathe as a work-holding and indexing fixture while you cut the reeds. As shown in *Flutes and Reeds*, flutes are small coves separated by flats, while reeds are half-round bead shapes divided by V-grooves.

Pencil-post beds and period table bases often have fluted and reeded columns. Chests of drawers, bookcases, and clocks often sport quarter- and half-columns with flutes or beads.

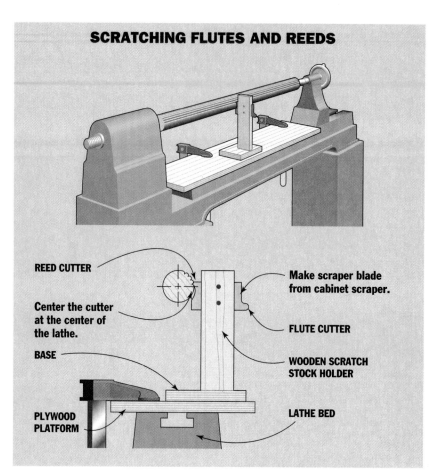

SCRATCHING FLUTES AND REEDS

REED CUTTER

Center the cutter at the center of the lathe.

BASE

PLYWOOD PLATFORM

Make scraper blade from cabinet scraper.

FLUTE CUTTER

WOODEN SCRATCH STOCK HOLDER

LATHE BED

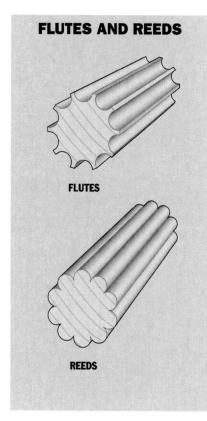

FLUTES AND REEDS

FLUTES

REEDS

Cutting Flutes and Reeds with a Scratch Stock

The shop-made scratch stock, discussed in "Making a Scratch Stock" on page 21, easily adapts to circular work. As shown in *Scratching Flutes and Reeds*, you just make a simple T-shaped scraper holder, mount a blade in it, and run it along a plywood platform that's clamped to the lathe bed. When you bolt the scraper blade into the scratch stock, pay attention to its cutting height. The center of the tool should be right at the center height of the lathe. This ensures the tool is cutting on a radius of the turning, so each flute or reed will be symmetrical. The lathe's indexing plate locks the workpiece in place while you scrape out the shapes.

Fluting and Reeding with the Router

For most people, the electric router has replaced the scratch stock as the tool of choice for adding flutes and reeds to turnings. To profile a column with the router, you will need to make a jig. "Box Jig for Routing Flutes and Reeds" shows a simple jig that works with straight and tapered columns. Screw but do not glue the L-shaped fence strips to the top of the box. You'll need to remove them to insert shim strips in order to customize the jig for different diameter turnings and varying degrees of taper. Standard groove-forming router bits will cut flutes or beads in a column, as shown in the drawing. Make each cut at top dead center.

SHOP SOLUTIONS: Box Jig for Routing Flutes and Reeds

This simple box jig will make fluting and reeding a turned cylinder easy, as shown in the drawing at right. It is a plywood box assembled with butt joints and drywall screws. The dimensions on the drawing are approximate and should be adjusted to fit your lathe, your router, and the size of the turnings you want to work with. The distance between the guide rails is critical, however—you want your router's baseplate to slide comfortably along the ledge cut into the rails.

STEP 1 Cut the parts to size.

STEP 2 Screw and glue the ends to the sides. Then screw and glue the sides and ends to the bottom.

STEP 3 Rout a $\frac{1}{2} \times \frac{1}{4}$-inch rabbet in each of the guide rails.

STEP 4 Screw the guide rails to the sides, but don't glue them. Shim one end higher than the other to flute or reed tapered cylinders.

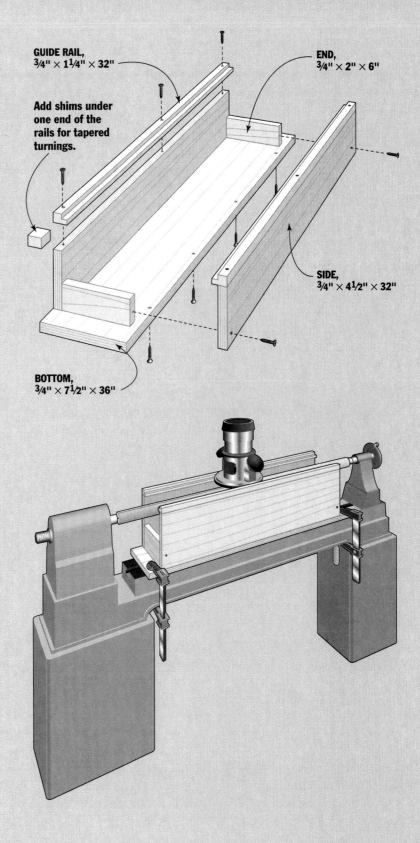

GUIDE RAIL, $\frac{3}{4}" \times 1\frac{1}{4}" \times 32"$

Add shims under one end of the rails for tapered turnings.

END, $\frac{3}{4}" \times 2" \times 6"$

SIDE, $\frac{3}{4}" \times 4\frac{1}{2}" \times 32"$

BOTTOM, $\frac{3}{4}" \times 7\frac{1}{2}" \times 36"$

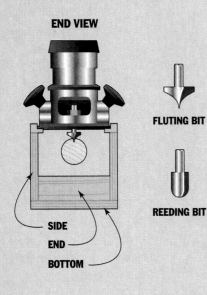

END VIEW

FLUTING BIT

REEDING BIT

SIDE

END

BOTTOM

Considering a Spindle Shaper

For many operations, the spindle shaper and the table-mounted router can be used interchangeably. Yet they are not the same machine. In general, the shaper can take a heavier cut and will produce a smoother and more accurate finish than the router table. For all of the router's versatility, there are many operations the shaper does better, and some operations—making curved handrails, for example—can only be done on the shaper. Above all, the shaper is a production machine that's capable of working all day long, a regimen that destroys high-speed routers.

The shaper consists of a cast-iron table, a spindle, and a motor mounted underneath. The cutters are locked onto the spindle, which adjusts up and down. The shaper is heavy—a commercial model weighs in north of 400 pounds, in the same class as a cabinet-grade table saw; see the photo on page 77.

Where the router spindle and motor comprise a single, straight-line unit, the shaper motor stands off to one side and drives the spindle by means of pulleys and belts. This arrangement makes space for a large, heavy motor, it permits speed adjustments by changing pulley sizes, and it puts the motor out of the pathway of chips and dust. It also separates the spindle bearings from the motor bearings.

Most shapers have two spindle speeds: one around 7,000 rpm, the other around 10,000 rpm. Compare that to the 22,000 rpm speed of routers. How can a shaper

Shaper cutters come in three basic styles: the safety head with inserted knives (top), standard three-wing cutters (bottom), and cutter sets (right), which can be assembled in various configurations for cope-and-stick or tongue-and-groove work.

produce a smoother surface if it runs at a slower speed? It does so by swinging a larger cutter than you ever could mount on a router. The velocity at the cutting edge is higher, despite the lower spindle speed. A 1-inch router cutter at 22,000 rpm delivers about the same rpm speed as a 3-inch shaper cutter at 7,000 rpm.

If you decide to add a shaper to your shop, you have to watch out for compromises masquerading as economies. Look for these features:

● Start with the table. It should be cast-iron, with a milled cross-feed slot. Look for a machine with a standard $3/4$-inch spindle. Many shapers have interchangeable spindles, with $3/4$ inch and $1 1/4$ inch being

the most common. The bigger the spindle, the more solidly the shaper will perform. A shaper that has only a $1/2$-inch spindle is too small. Look for a $1 1/2$-horsepower or larger motor.

● The fence should be a cast-iron assembly with separately adjustable infeed and outfeed sections. The center area of the fence assembly should have a fitting for dust collection.

● Shapers normally run counterclockwise, but good machines have a reversing switch, which allows you to change the feed direction. This can be a valuable safety feature. Sometimes you want to make a cut with the cutter underneath the wood—where it's safest—as opposed

PIN ROUTERS

Pin routers combine features of the router table and shaper. Like a shaper, they're heavily built with cast iron and have a large work table. But the operating motor is essentially a heavy-duty industrial router, and it accepts standard router bits.

The pin router is a pattern-following tool. In some versions, the router is mounted under the table, and in some it is mounted above it. Either way, there's a pattern-following guide pin directly over (or under) the router spindle. The key feature, however, is a foot-operated lever that moves the router up and down to engage the workpiece. Consequently, the machine can follow inside patterns as well as outside edge patterns. It can cut partway through the wood or all the way through. It can make a circle and a closed ring and can follow the intricate shapes of letters and numbers for sign making.

This small pin router is suitable for production pattern work. The pin traces a top-mounted pattern while the foot pedal moves the router spindle up into the workpiece. Thus you can start the cut in the center of the workpiece and follow an interior pattern.

to on top of the wood with the cutter exposed, and the only way you can do it is by reversing the cutter direction.

- On some shapers, the motor and spindle move up and down as a single unit. On others, the spindle moves while the motor remains stationary. It doesn't make any operational difference, provided the spindle can be locked in position without any deflection. Good machines have an adjustment to remove play from the mechanism, cheap machines do not.

Shaper Cutters

You'll find several styles of shaper cutters on the market, as shown in the photo on the opposite page. One style, known generically as three-wing cutters, has three wings cast onto a single mass of steel. These are sturdy, single-purpose cutters, available in the same range of shapes as router bits, only in much larger sizes. As with router bits, high-speed steel was once used but now carbide is the rule. Three-wing cutters also come in stacked sets for cutting more complex profiles, such as cope-and-stick door

cutters. With these, the individual cutters can be rearranged in numerous ways to make different profiles.

Commercial shops usually use a safety-head cutter system, which is a machined disk with slots that accept two inserted cutters or knives—much like the table-saw molding head. Safety head knives typically are made of high-speed steel, though carbide-tipped knives are also available. This system permits grinding pairs of knives to make custom profiles. It also requires meticulous attention to detail when setting up the cutterhead because a loose knife can be lethal.

Using the Shaper

As with any tool, the shaper can be quite dangerous if used improperly. Here are some key safety points to pay attention to:

- Always unplug the machine before you work on it. This goes for knife changes, too. Don't rely on the electrical switch—it's all too easy to bump it on while your attention is elsewhere.
- Lock the spindle height, tighten the spindle nuts, check that the knives are secure in their slots, and select the right speed. Then rotate the spindle by hand before you switch the motor on. Make sure the cutter rotates along with the spindle, and that nothing hangs up.
- Don't skimp on guards. You can always screw a protective piece of wood onto the fence, if necessary. A good guard is a visual reference as well as a finger shield. It shows you where the danger zone is, and it keeps your fingers out of danger.
- Don't try climb cuts on the shaper. Always feed the work against the direction of rotation.

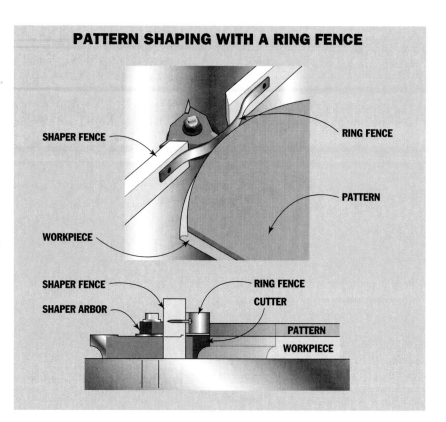

PATTERN SHAPING WITH A RING FENCE

SHAPER FENCE

RING FENCE

PATTERN

WORKPIECE

SHAPER FENCE

SHAPER ARBOR

RING FENCE

CUTTER

PATTERN

WORKPIECE

- Always bury the cutter in the fence, and avoid any setup where the work has to run in a trap between the cutter and the fence. Whenever possible, shape with the cutter below the work, rather than above it.
- Use jigs, featherboards, hold-downs and hold-ins. Part of the challenge of shaper work is devising safe jigs and setups.
- Don't shape small pieces,

warped pieces, or wood with knots. You'll only invite tear-out and kickback. When you need a little piece, shape it while it is attached to a big piece, then saw it off after shaping.

Shaper Setups

Once you've got a cutter securely mounted on the spindle, set up the fence. Most shapers come with a two-part adjustable fence. It works just like the split fence for the router table shown in *Split Fence for the Router Table* on page 23, only easier because each half of the fence is independently adjustable. When you are shaping the whole edge of the workpiece, adjust the split fence so the outfeed side is in line with the shallowest part of the cut, and the infeed side is set back by the depth of the cut. When you are shaping part of the edge, set the two halves of the fence in line with one another.

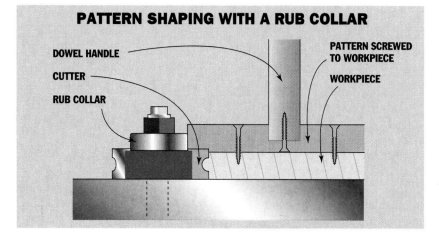

PATTERN SHAPING WITH A RUB COLLAR

DOWEL HANDLE

CUTTER

RUB COLLAR

PATTERN SCREWED TO WORKPIECE

WORKPIECE

For curved work, you need a pattern follower such as a ring fence or a rub collar. A ring fence can be any convex-curve–shaped attachment that the pattern can ride against. The simplest approach is to bend a piece of sturdy metal to the radius needed for a specific operation and attach it to the fence, as shown in *Pattern Shaping with a Ring Fence.*

A ring fence works fine for shaping shallow convex curves, but not for tight convex curves because the depth of cut will change slightly if you don't keep the curved edge of the workpiece centered on the cutter. You end up making multiple passes to correct for the inconsistent cut.

For tight curves, use a rub collar, which is a metal disk mounted on the spindle just above the cutter, as shown in *Pattern Shaping with a Rub Collar.* Some rub collars spin along with the cutter and tend to burn whatever they rub against. If you're using a pattern, that won't be too big a problem. But it will be if the edge of the workpiece itself is serving as the pattern. In this case,

you can use a ball-bearing rub collar. The only complication is finding the exact diameter you need.

Pattern shaping is like pattern routing, in that the workpiece is

attached to the pattern, which rides against a ring fence or rub collar. (See page 40) In shaper work, however, the pattern should be made of stock that is about ¾ inch thick. This permits you to attach the workpiece by screwing or nailing through the pattern. It's very helpful to mount handles onto the pattern, making it into a work-carrying fixture.

When starting a cut on a curved edge, always use a starting pin. As shown in "Using a Starting Pin," a starting pin acts as a pivot. You hold the workpiece against the pin, and then pivot it into the cutter. Once the workpiece contacts the follower, you pivot it off of the starting pin and make the cut. If you try to start a cut on a curved edge without a starting pin, the cutter may grab the wood and pull it from your hands, and it might pull your hand into the cutterhead. The starting pin is an important safety device.

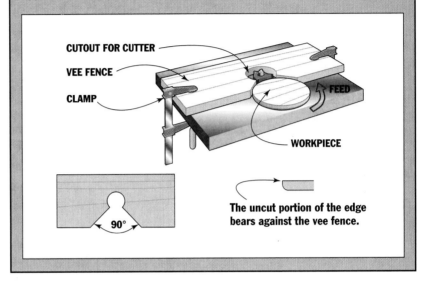

RIPPINGS

SHAPING DISCS ON THE SHAPER
When you want to shape the edge of a circular disk, you can clamp a vee fence to the shaper table, as shown in the drawing below. Note that the vee fence must bear on an unshaped portion of the edge of the workpiece to support the cut. It cannot be used to shape the complete edge in one pass.

CUTOUT FOR CUTTER
VEE FENCE
CLAMP
FEED
WORKPIECE

90°

The uncut portion of the edge bears against the vee fence.

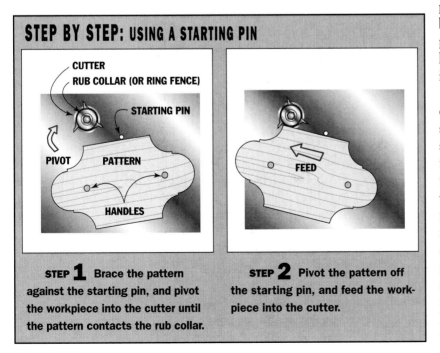

STEP BY STEP: USING A STARTING PIN

CUTTER
RUB COLLAR (OR RING FENCE)
STARTING PIN
PIVOT
PATTERN
HANDLES

FEED

STEP 1 Brace the pattern against the starting pin, and pivot the workpiece into the cutter until the pattern contacts the rub collar.

STEP 2 Pivot the pattern off the starting pin, and feed the workpiece into the cutter.

PUSHING THE LIMITS: Making Quarter Columns

Tall clocks and Queen Anne bureaus often sport quarter columns tucked into the corners of the case; see "A Compendium of Shapes" on page 3. They are moldings, except that they are turned on the lathe. They can be finished smooth, fluted, or beaded.

If you make a round turning and then saw it into quarters, you'll lose so much wood in the saw kerf that you'll end up with noticeably less than a quarter column. A better approach is to glue up four square sticks of wood, separated by a layer of newspaper or brown paper. Glue the sticks in pairs first, then glue the pairs together into the quartered square. After turning and then fluting or reeding, separate the column into quarters with no lost wood by driving a wide, bevel-edged chisel into the paper joint, as shown in **STEP 3** in "Making Quarter Columns."

Some craftsmen prefer quarter columns that have a little extra presence. They saw the fullness they want out of a complete turning, as shown in *Generous Quarter Columns*. It's safest to saw turnings in a vee cradle on the band saw.

GENEROUS QUARTER COLUMNS

Make a generous quarter column by sawing it in a vee cradle on the band-saw.

STEP BY STEP: MAKING QUARTER COLUMNS

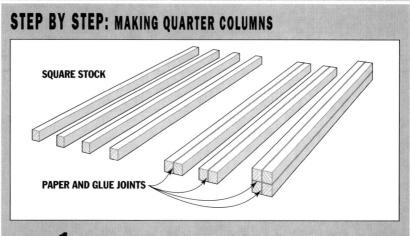

SQUARE STOCK

PAPER AND GLUE JOINTS

STEP 1 Prepare four equal lengths of square stock, and glue them together with a single layer of paper in each glue joint.

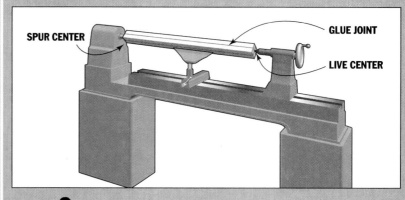

SPUR CENTER

GLUE JOINT

LIVE CENTER

STEP 2 Mount the turning blank onto the lathe, using a faceplate, then turn the cylinder to the required diameter.

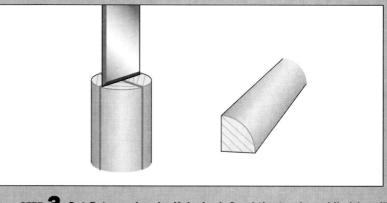

STEP 3 Cut flutes or beads, if desired. Sand the turning while it's still on the lathe, then remove the turning, and drive a wide chisel into the paper joints to separate the quarters.

PROJECTS

FOLDING SCREEN

A folding screen is a convenient way to divide today's open interiors into smaller, more intimate spaces. You might also use one to block off the tree from view on Christmas morning or as a background in the corner of a room.

This folding screen includes several shaping opportunities. Both the crest rail and the bottom rail are pattern-sawed and routed. And the applied bead, which holds the panels and mirror in place, must be profiled.

Once you've made the patterns, construction is quite straightforward. Make the frame from solid wood and the panels from a matching plywood. The rails are joined to the legs with mortise-and-tenon joints, and the beads are nailed and screwed in place. The only slightly tricky part is fitting the beads to the curved rails. While the pieces are probably thin enough to bend cold, you'll have better luck getting them to hold the curve if you steam them first. (This isn't as tough as it might sound; throwing the pieces in a pot of boiling water on a kitchen stove will work just fine.)

As a variation, you could build the screen without the mirror, espe-cially if you see it mostly as a room divider. Or you could build just a single section to hang as a full-length mirror. If you go this route, think about upgrading the glass to $\frac{1}{4}$ inch thick. The thicker glass gives a better reflection, but it is enough heavier that it would make the freestanding screen unstable and harder to move around. For a truly splendid dressing screen, include a mirror in all three framed sections.

EXPLODED VIEW

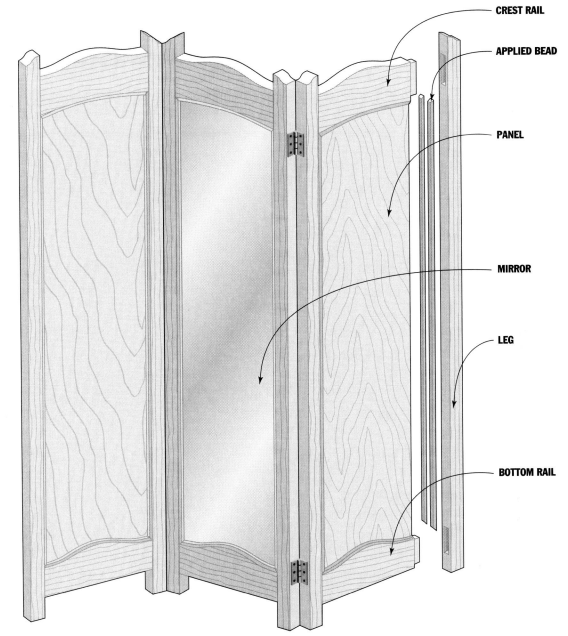

CREST RAIL

APPLIED BEAD

PANEL

MIRROR

LEG

BOTTOM RAIL

MATERIALS LIST

PART	QTY.	DIMENSIONS	HARDWARE	QTY.
Legs	6	$1\frac{1}{8}$" × $1\frac{3}{4}$" × 66"	$1\frac{1}{8}$" double-acting, folding screen hinges	3 pairs*
Crest rails	3	$1\frac{1}{8}$" × $5\frac{5}{8}$" × $15\frac{7}{8}$"	$\frac{1}{8}$" mirror, cut to fit opening	
Bottom rails	3	$1\frac{1}{8}$" × $3\frac{5}{8}$" × $15\frac{7}{8}$"	1" wire brads	+/-100
Panels ($\frac{1}{4}$ plywood)	3	$\frac{1}{4}$" × $13\frac{1}{2}$" × 56"	#4 × $\frac{3}{4}$" flat-head brass wood screws	20
Applied bead	10	$\frac{1}{4}$" × $\frac{7}{16}$" × 58"		
Applied mirror bead	5	$\frac{1}{4}$" × $\frac{3}{8}$" × 58"	*Available from the Woodworkers Store, (800) 279-4441, (Catalog #29041)	

Procedure

1 **Make the frames.** Cut the legs and rails to the sizes listed in the Materials List. Join the pieces with mortise-and-tenon joints, as shown in the *Front View* and the *Crest Rail Detail,* and *Bottom Rail Detail.*

The easiest way to cut the mortises is with a plunge router equipped with an edge guide and a $\frac{1}{2}$-inch straight bit, as shown in **Photo 1**. If you don't have a plunge router, lay out the mortises and drill out most of the waste. Then pare the mortises to size with a chisel.

Cut the tenons on the rails with the table saw. Make the shoulder cuts first with a fine crosscut blade on the saw. Guide the pieces with the miter gauge and use a stop block against the rip fence to position the cuts. You'll have to change the blade height to make the end cuts. Then switch to a rip blade and make the face cuts with the pieces held on end in a tenoning jig, as shown in **Photo 2**.

2 **Shape the rails.** Since there are three of each type of rail, it's worth taking the time to make templates of the two shapes. Cut the templates according to the *Crest Rail Detail* and the *Bottom Rail Detail.* Attach the templates to the rail pieces with double-sided carpet tape, then pattern-saw and pattern-rout the pieces to shape. While you're cutting the good pieces, cut an extra pair of rails from scrap wood to serve as forms over which to bend the pieces of applied bead.

3 **Assemble the frames.** While the pieces are still apart and easy to manage, mortise the hinges into the edges of the legs. The center frame gets hinges on both sides,

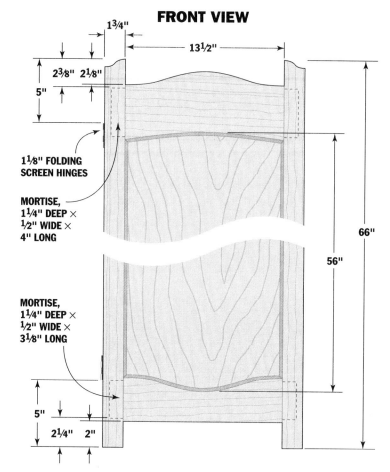

FRONT VIEW

1¾"
13½"
2³⁄₈" 2⅛"
5"
66"
56"

1⅛" FOLDING SCREEN HINGES

MORTISE, 1¼" DEEP × ½" WIDE × 4" LONG

MORTISE, 1¼" DEEP × ½" WIDE × 3⅛" LONG

5"
2¼" 2"

Photo 1 Lay out the ends of each mortise so you'll know exactly where to cut the mortise. Set the edge guide to center the bit on the stock. Plunge the ends of the mortise first, then clean out the middle in several passes.

the outer frames only on one. Then glue the frames together. Measure the diagonals to make sure the frames are square. (The two measurements should be equal.)

4 Cut the panels to size.

Cut the panels to the right width, but about ½ inch long to begin with. Set the frames on top of them, and trace the curved outlines at the top and bottom. Cut the panels to shape on the band saw. (Don't worry about being 100 percent accurate—because the edges are covered by the applied bead, close is good enough.) Once you have the panels cut, take one with you when you go to get the mirror. Most glass cutters like to work from a pattern.

5 Make the applied bead.

Make the pieces of applied bead from four strips of wood, ¼ inch thick × 2¼ inch wide × 58 inches long. Round-over both edges of each strip, then rip a bead to width off either edge on the table saw. Round-over the new edges of the strips, and rip them again. Each strip should make four beads. Be sure to make five of the beads narrower than the others to accommodate the mirror, as indicated in the Materials List.

6 Bend the beads. Cut three

of the beads (including one narrow one) into four equal lengths. These are the pieces that fit along the crest and bottom rails. Boil or steam the pieces for an hour to make them pliable. Don a pair of work gloves to protect your hands and fish the beads out two at a time with tongs. Bend them between the extra rails, and set them aside to dry, as shown in **Photo 3** on page 96. If possible, enlist an assistant to help you with this step. Allow the beads to dry overnight.

7 Inset the panels. Cut four

pieces of bead to fit around the

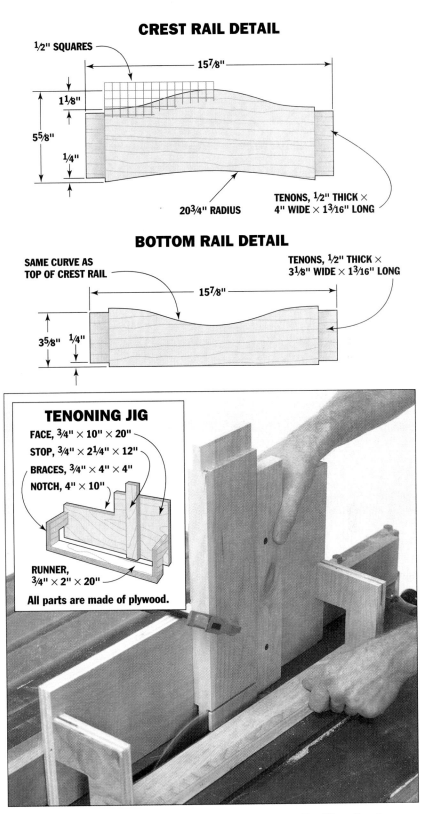

CREST RAIL DETAIL

½" SQUARES

15⁷⁄₈"

1⅛"

5⅝"

¼"

20¾" RADIUS

TENONS, ½" THICK × 4" WIDE × 1³⁄₁₆" LONG

BOTTOM RAIL DETAIL

SAME CURVE AS TOP OF CREST RAIL

TENONS, ½" THICK × 3⅛" WIDE × 1³⁄₁₆" LONG

15⁷⁄₈"

3⅝" ¼"

TENONING JIG

FACE, ¾" × 10" × 20"

STOP, ¾" × 2¼" × 12"

BRACES, ¾" × 4" × 4"

NOTCH, 4" × 10"

RUNNER, ¾" × 2" × 20"

All parts are made of plywood.

Photo 2 **Clamp the rails to the jig against the stop. Position the rip fence and make the first face cut on each of the rails. Then bump the fence over to make the second face cut on each piece. Make the end cuts with the rails held perpendicular to the jig face.**

inside of each frame. (Make sure to keep track of the narrow pieces.) Miter the pieces to fit together at the corners. Predrill the holes and nail the pieces to the frames, flush with one side, as shown in the *Leg Cross Section.* Space the nails 4 to 6 inches apart. On the mirrorless frames, drop the panels in place. Then miter four more pieces of bead to fit and nail them to the frames to trap the panels.

For the mirror frame, make up a 2-inch × 4-inch spacer, whose thickness equals the combined thickness of the mirror and its accompanying panel. Attach the second set of beads to the mirror frame with #4 × ¾-inch screws. Use the spacer to maintain the proper spacing. The spacer will allow you good access to the bead. If you try to drill the holes with the mirror in place, you may scratch or even break it.

8 **Finish up.** Remove the mirror-retaining beads. Do any touch-up sanding that is necessary to all parts of the screen. Pay special attention to the part of the beads that will be in contact with the mirror face—you'll be able to see any flaws reflected in the mirror.

Since the screen isn't likely to see heavy use, its finish needn't be especially bulletproof. An oil finish would be appropriate. Or, for a little more gloss, you might want to try shellac. It's easy to apply, dries quickly, and is relatively nontoxic. As a bonus, it is quite easy to repair should that ever be necessary. Once the finish dries, install the mirror and hinge the individual units together.

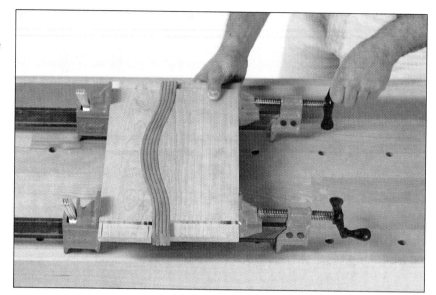

Photo 3 Remove the strips as quickly as you can from the steamer or boiler and stack them between the rails. Tighten the clamps to make the bends.

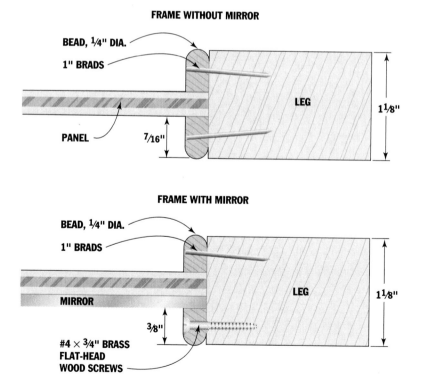

LEG CROSS SECTION

FRAME WITHOUT MIRROR

BEAD, ¼" DIA.

1" BRADS

LEG

PANEL

7/16"

1⅛"

FRAME WITH MIRROR

BEAD, ¼" DIA.

1" BRADS

MIRROR

LEG

3/8"

1⅛"

#4 × ¾" BRASS FLAT-HEAD WOOD SCREWS

FRAME-AND-PANEL NIGHTSTAND

Frame-and-panel construction dominates this traditionally styled cabinet, while the rich warmth of walnut completes a classic look.

This cabinet is proportioned to serve as either a nightstand or an end table. With some minor changes in the dimensions, it could easily become a hall table, a blanket chest, or even a sideboard—all the procedures would remain the same. No matter how you size it, the design employs five of the shaping techniques explored earlier in the book: raised panels, cope-and-stick joinery, curved rails, beading with a scratch stock, and beveling an edge on the table saw.

Like all cabinetry projects, this one can be simplified by breaking it down into smaller subassemblies. The basic unit of construction here is the frame-and-panel assembly. Sides, back, and doors are all made using identical cope-and-stick join-ery, but there are small differences to note. First, the top rails and the top edge of the panels on the doors are curved. This breaks the monotony of all the rectangular planes. And second, a plywood panel substitutes for a raised panel in the back, saving time and wood. These variations make the project more interesting and economical, without making it more difficult.

EXPLODED VIEW

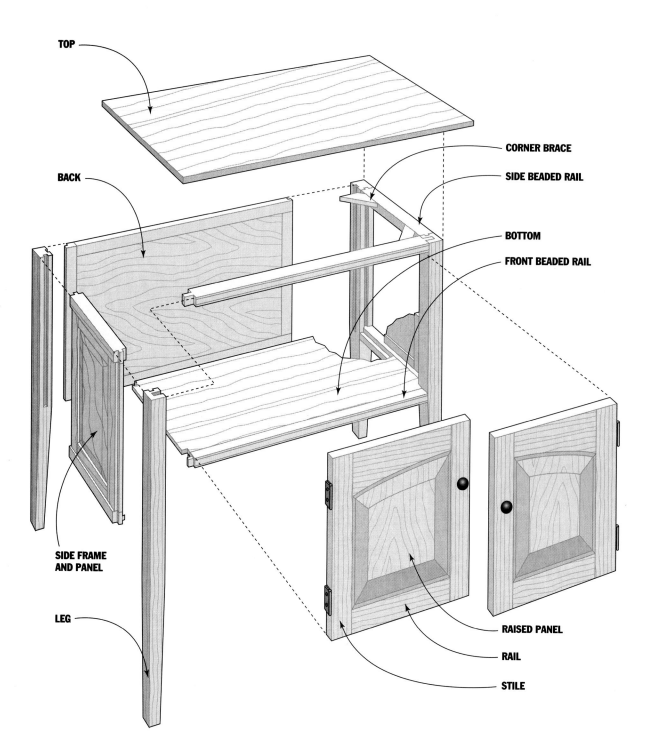

TOP

CORNER BRACE

SIDE BEADED RAIL

BACK

BOTTOM

FRONT BEADED RAIL

SIDE FRAME
AND PANEL

RAISED PANEL

RAIL

LEG

STILE

FRONT VIEW

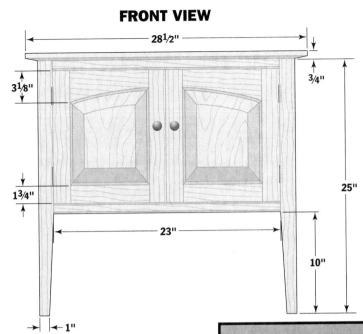

28½"

3¹⁄₈"

¾"

1³⁄₄"

25"

23"

10"

1"

SIDE VIEW

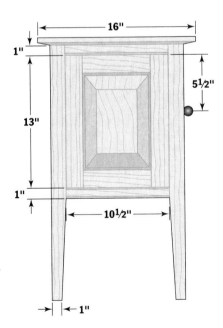

16"

1"

5½"

13"

1"

10½"

1"

MATERIALS LIST

PARTS	QTY.	DIMENSIONS
Top	1	¾" × 16" × 28½"
Legs	4	1½" × 1½" × 25"
Beaded side rails	4	1½" × 1" × 12½"
Beaded front rails	2	1½" × 1" × 25"
Side stiles	4	¾" × 2" × 13"
Side rails	4	¾" × 1¾" × 7¾"
Side panels	2	½" × 7⅝" × 10⅛"
Door stiles	4	¾" × 1¾" × 13"
Top door rails	2	¾" × 3½" × 8¾"
Bottom door rails	2	¾" × 1¾" × 8¾"
Door panels	2	½" × 8⅝" × 10⅛"
Back stiles	2	¾" × 2" × 15"
Back rails	2	¾" × 1¾" × 20¼"
Corner braces	4	¾" × 2½" × 6"
PLYWOOD PARTS		
Back	1	½" × 12⅛" × 20⅛"
Bottom	1	½" × 10½" × 24"
HARDWARE		
1½" × 2" brass butt hinges	4	
¾" solid brass spool pulls	2	
Small brass bullet catches	2	
#4 finish nails	As needed	
#8 × 1¼" round-head wood screws	4	

Procedure

1 **Cut all the parts to the sizes given in the Materials List.** You may want to leave the panels slightly oversize for now, and cut them to their final dimension after you've cut the joinery for the frames. (NOTE: Dimensions of rails and stiles are based on a cope-and-stick router cutter with a ³⁄₈-inch-deep profile. Cutter profiles vary, so check yours and adjust the dimensions accordingly.)

2 **Make the legs.** Lay out and cut the 10-inch × ½-inch tapers on two adjacent sides of each leg. (The tapers on all the legs face into the cabinet, while the outside faces remain square.) On a router table, rout the ³⁄₈-inch-wide × ¼-inch-deep stopped grooves in the legs. The grooves are centered in the legs so all the grooves can be routed with a single setup. The back legs get two grooves, the front legs get just one each, as shown in the *Exploded View.*

Cut the mortises in the front legs for the front rails, as shown in *Rail-Leg Joinery.* Like the shallow grooves, these mortises are centered in the stock and can be routed with the same router table setup. Raise the bit 1 inch high. The ⁷⁄₈-inch-long top mortises can be cut by setting a single stop to the left of the bit. Cutting the bottom mortises requires that you carefully lower the leg onto the bit and set a stop at each end of the fence to define the ³⁄₄-inch-long mortises. You may need to add a longer auxiliary fence to your router table to set the stops. Note that the lower edge of the bottom mortises are ⅛ inch above the top of the taper, as shown in *Joinery Details.*

3 **Make the beaded rails.** Make a simple scratch stock, as described on page 21, to cut a ³⁄₁₆-inch bead on the front and side

RAIL-LEG JOINERY

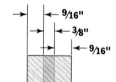

STUB TENON ON SIDE RAILS (TYP.)

1"

¼"

1"

3⁄8"

RIGHT FRONT LEG

SIDE RAILS

STOPPED GROOVE

FRONT RAILS

7⁄8"

½" × ½" **rabbet in the bottom rails receives the bottom.**

½" × ½" **NOTCH IN CORNERS OF BOTTOM**

½" **PLYWOOD BOTTOM**

3⁄4"

JOINERY DETAILS

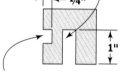

FRONT RAIL MORTISES

¼"

1"

GROOVE FOR SIDE RAILS AND SIDES

TOP FRONT RAIL, END VIEW

9⁄16"

3⁄8"

9⁄16"

⅛" **SHOULDER AT BOTTOM**

BOTTOM FRONT RAIL, END VIEW

⅛" **SHOULDERS ON TOP AND BOTTOM OF TENON**

10⅛" **TO BOTTOM EDGE OF MORTISE**

rails. Profile the bottom rails on both outside edges but bead the top rails only on their bottom outside edge—a bead on the top edge would be concealed by the top. Next, cut the tenons on the beaded rails. The two front rails get 1-inch-long tenons; the four side rails get ¼-inch-long tenons. Finally, cut the ½-inch × ½-inch rabbet on the inside of the three bottom rails to receive the bottom.

4 **Make the frame-and-panel assemblies.** Use a cope-and-stick router bit set in the router table to cut the profiles on the rails and stiles, as described in *Cope-and-Stick Joinery.* on page 49. After cutting the cope pattern in the ends of all the rails, lay out and cut the curve in the top rails of the doors, as shown in *Curved Door Rail, Cross Section, Typical Rail and Stile, and* "Routing a Cope-and-Stick Joint" on page 58. Since you need only two rails, you don't need to make a pattern—just strike the curve

Photo 1: *The most crucial thing about a frame-and-panel assembly is that it be glued up flat. Use two identical lengths of wood, jointed and planed on all four sides, to support the glue-up. Apply the clamps with the clamp screws centered on the stock.*

CURVED DOOR RAIL

After cutting a cope in the ends, saw the curve on the top door rails. Then use it as a pattern to trace the curve onto the door panels.

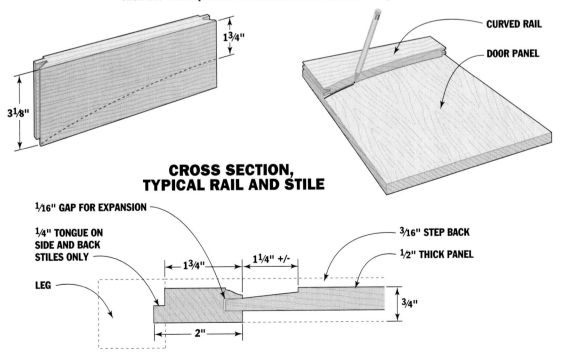

1¾"

3⅛"

CURVED RAIL

DOOR PANEL

CROSS SECTION, TYPICAL RAIL AND STILE

1/16" GAP FOR EXPANSION

¼" TONGUE ON SIDE AND BACK STILES ONLY

LEG

1¾"

1¼" +/-

3/16" STEP BACK

½" THICK PANEL

¾"

2"

SIDE SECTION

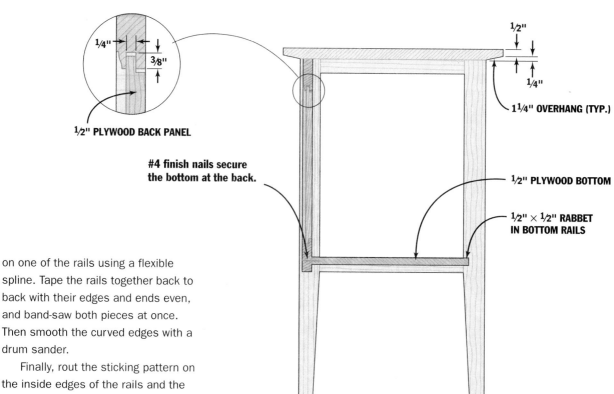

1/4" 3/8"

1/2" PLYWOOD BACK PANEL

#4 finish nails secure
the bottom at the back.

1/2" 1/4"

1 1/4" OVERHANG (TYP.)

1/2" PLYWOOD BOTTOM

1/2" × 1/2" RABBET
IN BOTTOM RAILS

on one of the rails using a flexible spline. Tape the rails together back to back with their edges and ends even, and band-saw both pieces at once. Then smooth the curved edges with a drum sander.

Finally, rout the sticking pattern on the inside edges of the rails and the stiles. You'll need to remove the fence and use the bearing guide to rout the curved rails, so do them last.

Raise the panels using one of the techniques discussed starting on page 54. Assemble the frames without glue and determine the exact dimensions of the panels. Allow $1/16$ inch on all sides of the panel for expansion due to any increase in moisture in the air. This means the panels are undersized by $1/8$ inch in both dimensions. Cut the panels and mold their edges with a panel-raising bit. Note that the back has a $1/2$-inch plywood panel, as shown in *Side Section.* You could just as well use solid raised panels if you have the wood. Sand all the panels thoroughly before assembling the frames, and consider applying at least a first coat of finish to them. That way if the panels shrink after assembly the wood

Photo 2: *Clamp the side frame-and-panel assembly and the side rails to the legs. The quick-action clamps help ensure a tight butt joint between the rails and the frame-and-panel assembly.*

revealed will have finish on it. Once the panels are sized for their frames, glue them up, as shown in **Photo 1** on page 101.

5 **Cut a tongue on the edges of the side and back assemblies.** Rout the ⅜-inch × ¼-inch rabbets to form the tongues. Make sure the tongue doesn't bottom out in the groove. The side and back frame and the panel assemblies are set back ³⁄₁₆ inch from the face of the rails.

6 **Glue up the side assemblies.** Assemble the side rails and side frame and panel assemblies to the legs without glue to be sure everything fits properly. There is no joint connecting the side rails to the side frame-and-panel assemblies—they just butt together. Apply clamps across the rails as shown in **Photo 2.**

7 **Make the bottom.** The bottom rests on the ½-inch × ½-inch rabbet in the front and side rails. Cut ½-inch × ½-inch notches at all four corners of the bottom so it will fit around the legs.

8 **Assemble the cabinet.** Assemble the cabinet dry to be sure everything fits properly. Do the glue-up on a flat level surface, and make sure all the legs touch the surface. Clamp across the front and back of the cabinet as shown in **Photo 3.** The bottom can be dropped into place after the main assembly. Support the back edge of the bottom with a few #4 finish nails through the back after assembly, as shown in *Side Section.*

9 **Attach the corner braces.** Corner braces strengthen the cabinet while providing a simple method for attaching the top. Cut the 45-degree miters on the ends of the 3-inch stock, then drill and countersink

Photo 3: *Measure across the diagonals and angle the clamps if necessary to pull the cabinet square. Otherwise you may find you're trying to hang doors in an out-of-square opening.*

⅛-inch holes through the mitered ends. Drill a ³⁄₁₆-inch hole through the center of each brace. The hole is intentionally larger than the screw that holds the top, which will allow the solid top to expand and contract slightly in relation to the cabinet.

10 **Make the top and attach it.** Cut the 12 degree bevel on the edge of the top on the table saw. Be sure to add a tall fence to keep the top stable as you make the cut. Attach the top to the cabinet with #8 × 1¼-inch round-head wood screws and washers.

11 **Hang the doors.** Measure the opening for the doors and trim the doors as necessary to create an even

gap of about ¹⁄₁₆ inch around each door. Mortise the doors and legs to receive the hinges—each hinge is located 1⅜ inches in from the edge of the door. Note that, unlike the back and sides, the doors are set flush with the face of the legs and rails.

12 **Install bullet catches.** Drill the appropriate-sized hole in the top edge of each door, and insert the bullet half of the catch. Locate the catch in the top rail, drill the hole for it, and nail it in place.

13 **Finish the cabinet.** Walnut shines beautifully with oil-based finishes. For this project, a wipe-on varnish or similar product would be ideal.

ACCENT LAMP

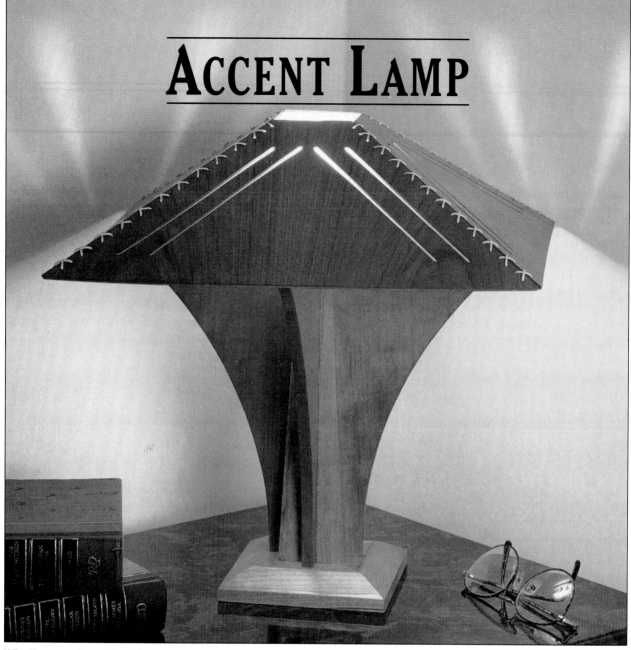

Whether used on a bedside table or a desk, this lamp is designed to provide soft, distinctive light, right where you need it.

There's nothing like putting just the right light on a particular subject, and this small table lamp will find many places to brighten and enhance in your home. Use it as a night-light on a hall table, or as a task light on a work desk.

The lamp is easy to make—the base requires just a few small pieces of hardwood, and the shade is made from ⅛-inch hardwood-faced ply-wood stitched together with nylon cord. I used cherry—it reflects light with such a warm glow—but other light woods like oak or maple would also be attractive. The hardware for the light is uncomplicated as well and should be available at your local hardware store. The shade is held to the base with tabs of Velcro.

The lamp is designed to produce a soft, low light with a 40-watt accent flood bulb, as shown in *Wiring and Hardware Details* on page 108. You could also use a lower wattage decorative bulb. If you want the convenience of using a standard-size bulb, stick to a 60-watt bulb or less to prevent heat buildup on the wooden shade. Because standard bulbs are a bit taller, you'll need to use the taller shade support, as shown in *Shade Support Details* on page 107.

EXPLODED VIEW

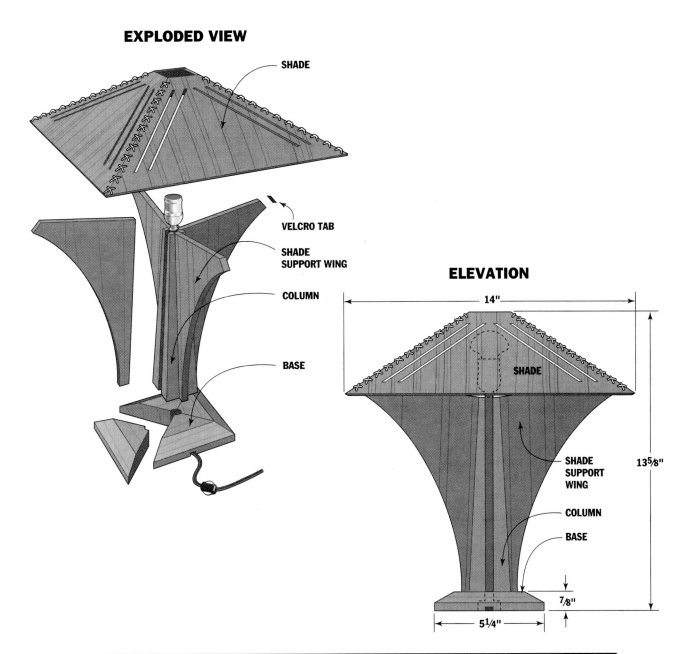

SHADE

VELCRO TAB

SHADE
SUPPORT WING

COLUMN

BASE

ELEVATION

14"

SHADE

SHADE
SUPPORT
WING

COLUMN

BASE

13⅝"

⅞"

5¼"

MATERIALS LIST

PART	QTY.	DIMENSIONS	HARDWARE	QTY.
Column halves	2	$1" \times 2" \times 9"$*	Lamp holder (socket)	1
Shade support wings	4	$\frac{3}{8}" \times 6" \times 10"$	#1 mason's nylon cord for shade	16'
Base	4	$\frac{7}{8}" \times 2\frac{5}{8}" \times 30"$	$\frac{1}{2}" \times \frac{1}{2}"$ Velcro tabs	4
Shade (⅛" hardwood-faced plywood)	4	$\frac{1}{8}" \times 7" \times 14"$	8' lamp cord set (includes on-off switch)	1
			$\frac{3}{8}" \times 10"$ threaded lamp rod	1
			Lamp rod nuts	2

*Leave oversize, and cut to final dimensions
  after assembling column halves;
  see *Column Details* on page 106.

Procedure

1 **Make the column blank.** The column is pyramidal in shape—tapered on all four sides. Start by cutting the two halves of the column slightly oversize in width and thickness and a few inches over the finished length. Rout or saw the groove along the center of the column halves to accept the threaded lamp rod. The lamp rod serves as a channel for the lamp cord, while the rod's outside threads allow you to bolt the base and the socket to the column. Be sure to test the fit of the rod in the groove before gluing the halves together; see *Column Details.* It should slide through the opening easily when the pieces are clamped together. Glue the column halves together, and crosscut the blank to 9 inches.

2 **Shape the column.** Taper the column—I prefer laying out the taper right on the workpiece, and band-sawing just outside of the lines. Lay out the taper working from the center of the column, not the edges. This way the tapers will be centered without needing to joint and plane the blank to finished dimensions first. You could also tablesaw the tapers with a tapering jig. Either way, you'll need to clean up the sawn surfaces. A belt sander will do the job on table-sawn tapers, but I prefer the jointer for band-sawn tapers because it's quicker and more accurate. The column is pretty short so be extra careful if you joint it; see **Photo 1.** Rout the grooves down the center of each face of the column for the shade support wings, as shown in **Photo 2.**

3 **Cut and shape the shade support wings.** The curved wings support the lamp shade and give the design a sense of upward lift. Plane the stock for the wings so it fits the grooves in the column. Make a pattern, as shown in *Shade Support Details,* and

COLUMN DETAILS

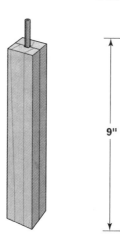

CENTERLINE

9"

Check the fit of the threaded lamp rod in the groove before gluing up the column halves.

Lay out the taper using a centerline.

Rout 3/16" deep × 3/8" wide grooves in each face of the column.

3/8" × 3/16" GROOVES FOR THREADED LAMP ROD

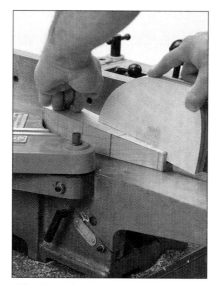

COLUMN HALVES, 1 1/16 × 2 1/8" × 12"

3/8" × 10" THREADED LAMP ROD

Photo 1: Because they're so short, be extra careful jointing the faces of the column. Set the jointer for a light cut, and pass the wood slowly over the cutter using a push block. Lead with the thick end of the column.

Photo 2: Rout the groove for the wings in a single pass. Use a 1/2-inch spacer at the narrow end of the column to compensate for the taper. The push block keeps the spacer from slipping out of place.

SHADE SUPPORT DETAILS

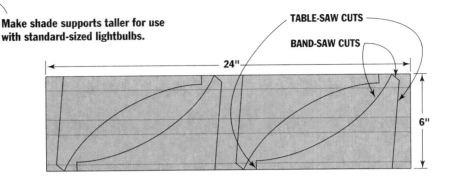

Make shade supports taller for use with standard-sized lightbulbs.

95°

9"

93°

9/16"   1 SQUARE=1/2"

Make a pattern for the shade support wing from 1/8" plywood.

6"

TABLE-SAW CUTS

BAND-SAW CUTS

24"

6"

Lay out the four supports on your stock. Make all of the 95° top cuts first on the table saw. Then band-saw the supports from the longer stock. Finally, make the 93° bottom cuts on the table saw.

use it to trace the shape of the wings on the stock. Use the straight edge of the stock as the back edge of the wings, and follow the sequence of cuts shown in the drawing. Note that when you make the table-saw cuts, the miter gauge is set to 5 degrees for the top edge of the support wings, then changed to 3 degrees for the bottom edge cut. Smooth the curves with a curved sanding block or with a drum sander on the drill press. (If you're making more than one lamp, consider using the pattern-sawing and pattern-sanding techniques described in Chapter 3, beginning on page 34.

4 Make the base. Shape the base molding as one long strip, then miter the individual pieces to length after shaping. Cut the stock for the base molding to the width and thickness listed in the Materials List. Bevel the molding with the stock on edge and the table-saw blade tilted to 33 degrees. On some saws, this will require that you move the fence to the left side of the blade. Sand the bevel smooth, then cut the blank into four, 5¼-inch-long pieces. Saw or rout a slot across the center of one of the mitered base pieces for the lamp cord, as shown in *Base Molding Details.* Add biscuits or splines to strengthen the

BASE MOLDING DETAILS

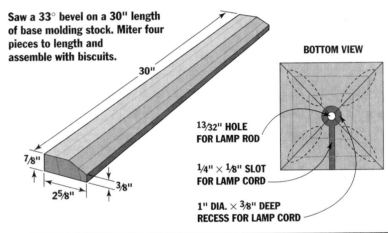

Saw a 33° bevel on a 30" length of base molding stock. Miter four pieces to length and assemble with biscuits.

30"

7/8"

2⅝"   3/8"

BOTTOM VIEW

13/32" HOLE FOR LAMP ROD

1/4" × 1/8" SLOT FOR LAMP CORD

1" DIA. × 3/8" DEEP RECESS FOR LAMP CORD

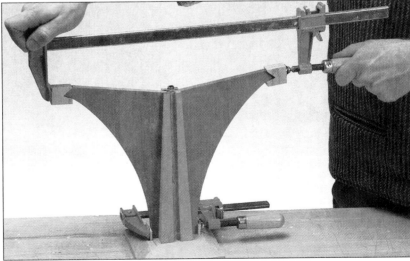

Photo 3: **Shape a block to fit around the top of the wings to give the clamp a square surface to grab. The wings are pretty delicate so don't overclamp them. Be sure the bottom of the wings sits flat on the base.**

miter joints, then clamp the pieces together with a band clamp.

After the glue sets, drill a 1-inch-diameter × ⅜-inch-deep recess into the bottom of the base at the center. This gives you room to tighten the lamp rod nut and allows the lamp cord to make a comfortable 90-degree turn. Drill a ¹³⁄₃₂-inch hole the rest of the way through the base for the threaded lamp rod.

5 **Glue the wings to the column.** First, bolt the assembled base molding to the column with the threaded lamp rod and nuts. There should be about ¼ inch of the rod accessible at the top of the column for the lamp socket. Align the corners of the column with the joint lines in the base, and tighten the bolts. Clamp and glue the wings into the column two at a time, as shown in **Photo 3** on page 107.

6 **Assemble the lamp hardware.** Pass the lamp wire up through the base and column so there are a few inches exposed at the top. Disassemble the lamp socket, screw the bottom half onto the end of the threaded lamp rod, and insert the set screw. Make the wire connections as shown in *Wiring and Hardware Details,* and reassemble the lamp socket.

7 **Make the shade.** Cut the plywood pieces to the size listed in the Materials List. Orient the face grain across the short dimension of the pieces so it will run vertically on the finished shade. Set the miter gauge to 40 degrees, and cut one end of each piece with the face side up. To make the second cut with the face side up, you'll need to reset the miter gauge to 40 degrees in the opposite direction. Set a stop on the miter-gauge fence, and make the second cut with the workpiece on the other side of the blade.

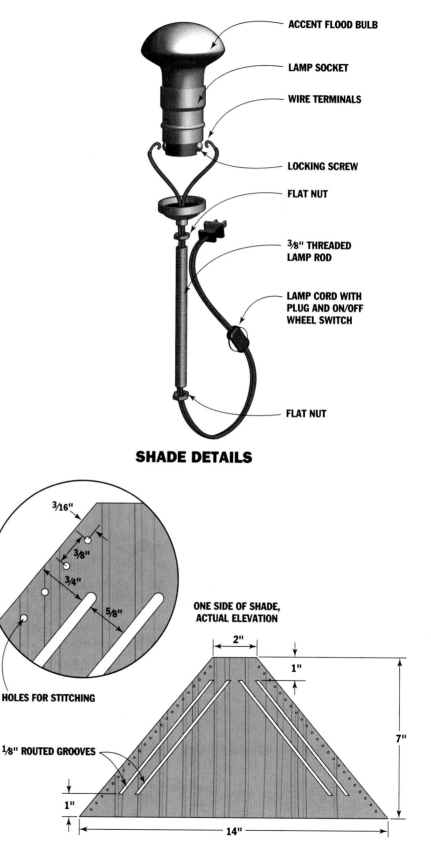

WIRING AND HARDWARE DETAILS

- ACCENT FLOOD BULB
- LAMP SOCKET
- WIRE TERMINALS
- LOCKING SCREW
- FLAT NUT
- ⅜" THREADED LAMP ROD
- LAMP CORD WITH PLUG AND ON/OFF WHEEL SWITCH
- FLAT NUT

SHADE DETAILS

3/16"
3/8"
3/4"
5/8"

HOLES FOR STITCHING

ONE SIDE OF SHADE, ACTUAL ELEVATION

2"
1"
7"
1"
14"

⅛" ROUTED GROOVES

Rout the four $\frac{1}{8}$-inch stopped slots along the angled edges of each shade piece, according to the dimensions in *Shade Details,* and as shown in **Photo 4.** Use a carbide bit in a router table. Lay out the slots directly on one of the shade pieces (or on a pattern if you want to be extra safe). Rout all the outside slots first, readjust the fence, mark new start and stop lines, and then rout the inside slots.

On a drill press, drill a row of $\frac{5}{64}$-inch diameter holes along the angled edges of the shade pieces; see *Shade Details.* Tape all four shade pieces together with clear packing tape so all the edges are aligned, and clamp a fence to the drill press table. The size of the holes and the spacing shown in the drawing are based on the type of cord used to thread the shade together. I used #1 mason's nylon line, which is about $\frac{1}{32}$ inch in thickness.

Finish sand both surfaces of the shade pieces, and round-over all the edges. Give them a coat of finish before stitching up the shade. Stitch together the shade using a simple shoelace pattern, as shown in **Photo 5** and **Photo 6**. The shade will be flimsy until you stitch the last seam.

8 **Apply a finish to the lamp and shade.** Because of its shape and size, this project is best finished with a spray. I used clear, semi-gloss spray lacquer. Apply at least three light coats, sanding between coats with #400 grit wet/dry paper.

9 **Affix the Velcro shade tabs.** Velcro is available in assorted sizes and shapes. You need only about 2 square inches. Cut pieces of Velcro to fit the ends of the shade support wings —or use ready-cut circular discs—and tape them in place. Carefully lower the shade onto the Velcro tape, looking down into the center opening to center the shade on the support wings.

Photo 4: **Use the leading point of each shade piece as the reference for starting (*top*) and stopping the cuts, (*bottom*) and mark the stop and start points on the fence. One set of slots is routed with the face side up and the other with the face side down.**

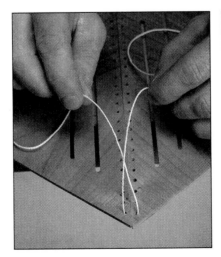

Photo 5: **String the pieces of the shade together like a shoelace, working from the bottom to the top with the pieces lying flat.**

Photo 6: **To keep the stitching tight, tie it off after every three sets of holes, and start a new piece. Cut the tied ends about $\frac{1}{4}$ inch from the knot with scissors.**

CLASSICAL BOOKCASE

Made from birch plywood with solid wood trim, this sturdy bookcase will hold dozens of books and still leave room for displaying photos, collectibles, and knickknacks.

Books make any room a more welcome place to spend time. This classically styled bookcase will give home to a ton of books, while making the room it's in more pleasant and organized. The five shelves are all adjustable to accommodate books of any height. The plywood shelves are edged with a stout band of solid wood to ensure they won't sag no matter what you load onto them. Though you'll need a few pieces of hardwood for the trim, the bookcase is made primarily from ¾-inch birch plywood, which is strong, inexpensive, and easy to work with. It paints well, too.

The sides of the bookcase are 3 inches thick, a feature that gives the cabinet aesthetic as well as structural strength. They're made by sandwiching two lengths of 1½-inch-thick blocking between two layers of ¾-inch plywood, and then capping the assembly with the solid wood pilasters. Building this project gives you many opportunities to practice shaping. There are fluted pilasters, a base molding and base cap, a coved crown and bullnosed crown cap, and an arched rail, which has an applied cove molding that continues around the sides of the cabinet. All the shaping techniques involved have been covered earlier in the book.

Procedure, Part 1: Make the Case

1 Cut the parts to the sizes listed in the Materials List on page 113. All the plywood parts can be cut from two 4 × 8 sheets. Refer to the *Side Cross Section* and *Front, Top,* and *Side View* drawings on page 113. Mill the solid wood parts to thickness and width, but leave them long for now and cut them to length as you go. That way you can use the case itself to determine their exact length.

2 Cut dadoes for the shelf standards. Set up a dado cutter on your table saw, and dado the case sides for the shelf pilasters. Set the fence so the edge of the dado is 1¼ inch from the edge of the side. Rather than try to set the dado for the exact width you need, set it somewhat narrower, and make the dado in two passes, resetting the fence in between. This way you avoid fiddling with shims to get the dado blade set just right. If you don't have a dado blade, a router with an edge guide or a router table will also work.

3 Assemble the case. Attach the top and bottom to the case sides with biscuit joints, as shown in the *Exploded View* on page 112. Note that the top and bottom extend ¾ inch beyond the sides at the front, making them even with the pilasters. The base cap molding and crown transition molding will cover these plywood edges. Predrill the case sides for screws. Then glue and screw the case together. The screws act as clamps to hold the pieces together while the glue dries. Since the case will be fairly flimsy until the back is attached, you may want to tack some diagonal braces to its back edges to keep it from racking as you work on it.

4 Attach the wall blocking and finished sides. Glue and clamp two

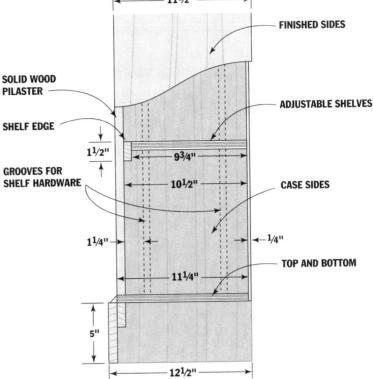

SIDE CROSS SECTION

WIDTHS OF PLYWOOD CASE PARTS

- SOLID WOOD PILASTER
- SHELF EDGE
- GROOVES FOR SHELF HARDWARE
- FINISHED SIDES
- ADJUSTABLE SHELVES
- CASE SIDES
- TOP AND BOTTOM

11½"
1½"
9¾"
10½"
1¼"
¼"
11¼"
5"
12½"

lengths of wall blocking to each cabinet side, making sure they are flush with the front and back edges of the sides. Predrill and screw the blocking to the cabinet sides using 2-inch drywall screws. Then glue and clamp the finished sides to the blocking, making sure the front edges of all the parts are flush. (The finished sides should extend ½ inch beyond the rear blocking.) To hasten the process, you can use screws to attach the finished sides to the blocking, then plug the screw holes.

5 Attach the back. Draw a line along each long edge of the back ¾ inch in from the edge—this will center the screws in the blocking. Predrill ⅛-inch-diameter holes 8 inches apart. Also drill holes along the top and bottom of the back, ⅜ inch in from the edges. Lay the cabinet face down and position the back. Drive #6 × ¾-inch screws along

one long edge first, then measure the diagonals to make sure the case is square. Square, if necessary, then drive screws in the rest of the holes.

Procedure, Part 2: Make the Arched Rail

Making the arched rail and the curved cove molding are the hardest parts of the project, but they also yield the most distinctive features of the bookcase. Proceed carefully and the results will be accurate and well worth the effort.

In a nutshell, to complete this part of the project, you need to use a router trammel to cut the curve in the arched rail. Then, you need to make a piece of cove molding whose inside radius follows the same curve as the one you

EXPLODED VIEW

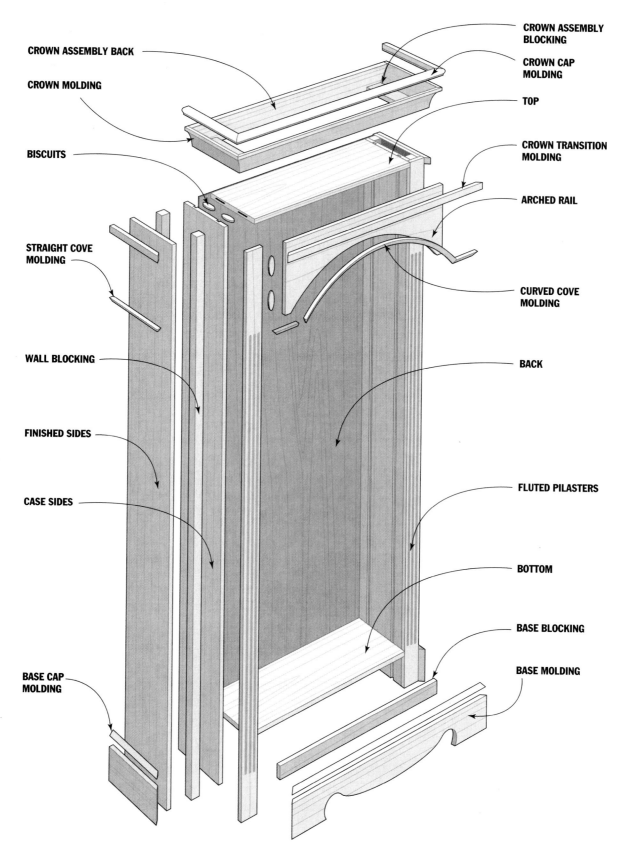

CROWN ASSEMBLY BACK

CROWN MOLDING

CROWN ASSEMBLY BLOCKING

CROWN CAP MOLDING

TOP

CROWN TRANSITION MOLDING

BISCUITS

ARCHED RAIL

STRAIGHT COVE MOLDING

CURVED COVE MOLDING

WALL BLOCKING

BACK

FINISHED SIDES

CASE SIDES

FLUTED PILASTERS

BOTTOM

BASE BLOCKING

BASE CAP MOLDING

BASE MOLDING

FRONT, TOP, AND SIDE VIEWS

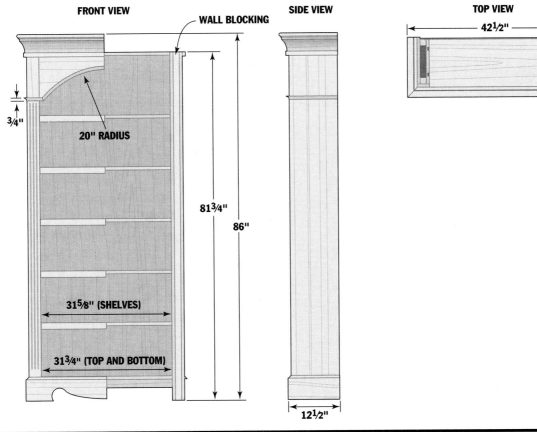

FRONT VIEW

WALL BLOCKING

3/4"

20" RADIUS

81 3/4"

86"

31 5/8" (SHELVES)

31 3/4" (TOP AND BOTTOM)

SIDE VIEW

12 1/2"

TOP VIEW

42 1/2"

MATERIALS LIST

SOLID WOOD PARTS*	QTY.	DIMENSIONS
Wall blocking	4	1½" × 1½" × 81¾"
Fluted pilasters	2	¾" × 3" × 81¾"
Arched rail	1	¾" × 9¼" × 31¾"
Crown molding	1	¾" × 4¼" × 84"
Crown assembly back	1	¾" × 3¼" × 42"
Crown assembly blocking	2	¾" × 3" × 12"
Crown cap molding	1	¾" × 1½" × 72"
Crown transition molding	1	¾" × 1" × 72"
Curved cove molding blank	1	¾" × 10½" × 31¾"
Straight cove molding	1	¾" × ¾" × 48"
Base molding	1	¾" × 5" × 72"
Base cap molding	1	⅝" × ⅝" × 72"
Shelf edges	6	¾" × 1½" × 31⅝"

*Leave all the solid wood parts long, and cut to final length as you go.

PLYWOOD PARTS	QTY.	DIMENSIONS
Case sides	2	¾" × 10½" × 81¾"
Finished sides	2	¾" × 11" × 81¾"
Top and bottom	2	¾" × 11¼" × 31¾"
Shelves	5	¾" × 9¾" × 31⅝"
Base blocking	1	¾" × 2" × 31¾"
Back	1	¼" × 36¼" × 76¾"

HARDWARE

Shelf pilasters	4
Shelf clips	20
2" drywall screws	As needed
1¼" screws	As needed
#6 × ¾" screws	As needed
#4 Finish nails	As needed
#20 Biscuits	12

cut in the rail. The easiest way to do this is to rout the same curve in two pieces of stock—in effect, you're routing two arched rails, then sawing what will become the applied cove molding from one of them. Next, you glue the molding to the rail, miter the ends, and rout a cove in it. Finally, you join the rail to the fluted pilasters, making a face frame, then attach the assembled trim to the cabinet.

1 Set up a trammel platform.
Start by cutting the blanks for the top rail and the curved cove molding to finished length—they should be identical in length to the interior width of the cabinet. Next, make a jig by cutting a scrap piece of plywood to 31¾ inches square, and tacking a 2-inch-wide cleat to one end, as shown in *Making the Arched Rail and Molding*. This will serve as the platform for making both trammel cuts.

2 Find the pivot point for the trammel. Clamp the rail blank to the plywood platform, as shown in the drawing, and draw layout lines 1 inch in from each end of the rail blank. These lines mark the end points of the curve. Use a set of trammel points set for a 20-inch radius to roughly find the pivot point for the router trammel. Screw a block about 8 inches square and ¾ inches thick at the pivot point to raise the pivot point to the same level as the workpiece. Then strike two arcs onto the pivot block from the end points that you marked on the rail—the pivot point for your trammel is at the intersection of these two arcs. Drill an ⅛-inch hole at the pivot point.

3 Rout the arcs on the rail and molding blank. Make a simple router trammel by attaching a router to a piece of ¼-inch plywood, as shown in *Making the Arched Rail and Molding*. Drill an ⅛-inch hole in the plywood 20 inches from the far side of the bit. Use

MAKING THE ARCHED RAIL AND MOLDING

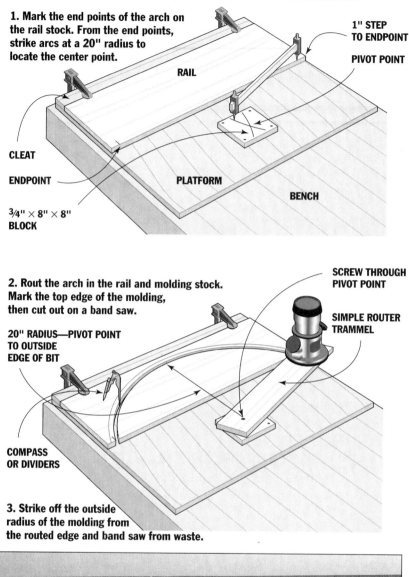

1. Mark the end points of the arch on the rail stock. From the end points, strike arcs at a 20" radius to locate the center point.

RAIL

1" STEP TO ENDPOINT

PIVOT POINT

CLEAT

ENDPOINT

PLATFORM

BENCH

¾" × 8" × 8" BLOCK

2. Rout the arch in the rail and molding stock. Mark the top edge of the molding, then cut out on a band saw.

SCREW THROUGH PIVOT POINT

20" RADIUS—PIVOT POINT TO OUTSIDE EDGE OF BIT

SIMPLE ROUTER TRAMMEL

COMPASS OR DIVIDERS

3. Strike off the outside radius of the molding from the routed edge and band saw from waste.

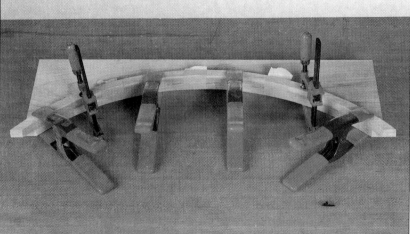

Photo 1: **Use spring clamps or small bar clamps to glue the curved molding to the arched rail.**

this hole to screw the plywood to the pivot point. Rout the arcs using a ½-inch bit—spiral flutes leave a smoother edge than straight flutes. Make three passes to get through the full ¾-inch thickness of each piece.

4 **Saw off the curved molding.** Use dividers or a compass with points set ¾ inch apart to mark off the outside radius of the curved molding, as shown in the drawing. Band-saw the curve carefully just outside the line. Smooth it with a plane and sanding block, using the line as a reference.

5 **Glue the curved molding to the arched rail.** Glue and clamp the curved molding stock to the arched rail, as shown in **Photo 1.** You want the inside edges to be perfectly flush, but the parts tend to squirm around when you clamp them. Start out with just hand pressure and strips of masking tape holding the two parts together. Let the glue tack up for a couple minutes then apply the clamps from the center out toward the ends. The molding should extend 1 inch or so beyond the bottom edge of the rail.

6 **Rout and miter the curved cove molding.** Before routing the cove on the molding, transfer the miter angle from the end of the curve on the rail, as shown in **Photo 2.** (Once you rout the cove, there's no material over which to convey the line.) Mount a ⅝-inch-radius cove-cutting bit with a ball-bearing guide in your router. Use the waste piece from the curved molding as a platform for the router to ride on, as shown in **Photo 3.** You may need to climb cut one side of the molding, from the end into the center, to avoid chip out. With the cove routed, miter the ends of the molding. Use the sliding bevel gauge set at 67.5 degrees to guide the cut with a handsaw, as shown in **Photo 4** and in *Mitering the Curved Cove Molding.*

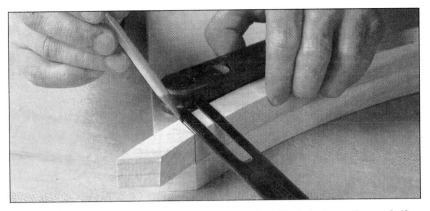

Photo 2: Use a square and bevel gauge set at 67.5 degrees to mark the miter on the molding.

Photo 3: Rout the cove in two or three passes with a bearing-guided bit. The waste pieces from the rail and curved molding helps balance the router on the thin edge of the molding when routing the cove.

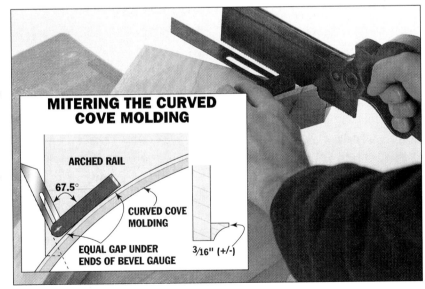

MITERING THE CURVED COVE MOLDING

ARCHED RAIL

67.5°

CURVED COVE MOLDING

EQUAL GAP UNDER ENDS OF BEVEL GAUGE

3/16" (+/-)

Photo 4: Use a bevel gauge to guide your handsaw as you miter the molding.

Procedure, Part 3: Finish the Trim, and Make the Shelves

1 Rout and miter the straight cove molding. Use the same router bit to shape the straight piece of cove molding, but put it into a router table. Work the short front pieces first, then the side pieces. The end of the front piece gets cut at a 67.5-degree angle where it meets the end of the curved molding. Attach the molding with finish nails.

2 Rout the flutes in the pilasters. Strike lines across each pilaster where the flutes will end, as shown in *Fluted Pilaster Details*. Mount a ⅜-inch core-box bit in your router, and attach an edge guide. Set the edge guide ⅝ inch from the edge of the bit for the outside flutes. Rout the two outside flutes on each pilaster, then reposition the edge guide for the center flutes.

3 Glue the arched rail between the pilasters. Note that the top of the rail is offset ¾ inch down from the top of the pilaster to make room for the top of the bookcase. Since clamping this assembly will be a bit awkward, lay the cabinet on its back on a set of sawhorses, and do the glue-up right on the cabinet.

4 Glue the pilaster/rail assembly to the cabinet. Once the glue dries, remove the clamps, and glue and clamp the pilasters to the cabinet. Align the inside edges of each pilaster with the inside face of the cabinet side. This way, if the pilasters overhang at all (this could happen if the plywood is slightly less than ¾ inch thick) the overhang will be on the outside of the case where it is easy to trim. The top of the cabinet extends out over the arched rail—this joint can be screwed

FLUTED PILASTER DETAILS

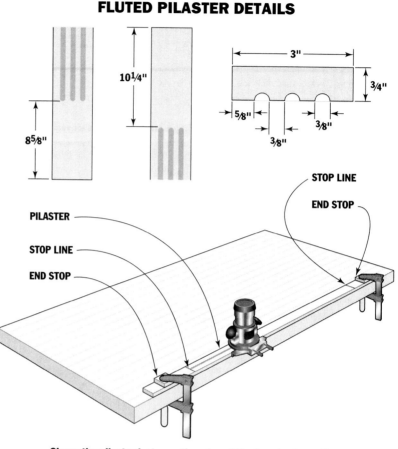

Clamp the pilaster just over the edge of the bench, clamp the end stops in place, and rout the flutes using an edge guide.

BASE MOLDING DETAILS

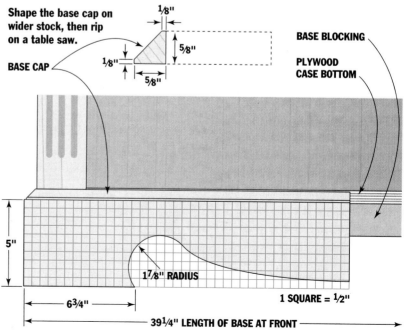

Shape the base cap on wider stock, then rip on a table saw.

or nailed together. The seam between the two parts gets covered by the crown transition molding.

5 **Attach the base blocking piece.** Cut this piece to fit between the pilasters. Glue and clamp it to the underside of the bottom so the face of the base blocking is even with the front edge of the case bottom.

6 **Make and attach the base molding.** Lay out the pattern in the front piece of base molding, as shown in *Base Molding Detail,* and cut it on the band saw. Miter the ends of the front piece, and nail it in place. Fit the side pieces of base molding by mitering their front ends, and then square cutting the back ends flush with the finish sides. Attach the base molding with #4 finish nails and glue.

Make the base-cap molding by routing a 45-degree bevel on the edge of the stock. For safety, rout the edge profile on wider stock, then rip it to finished size on the table saw. Go through the same sequence to cut and attach the base-cap molding as you did with the base molding.

7 **Attach the crown transition molding.** This rectangular molding wraps around the top of the case, covering the raw front edge of the plywood case top; see the *Exploded View.* Miter the corners and secure the pieces to the case, with #4 finish nails and glue, making sure that the top edge of the molding is flush with the top of the case.

8 **Make and attach the crown molding.** Cut the cove in the crown stock on the table saw by setting a fence at a 62-degree angle to the blade. Smooth the cove while the stock is still square, then rip both edges of the molding with the blade set to a 28-degree angle, as indicated in *Crown Molding Details.* The flat listel that faces frontward should be

CROWN MOLDING DETAILS

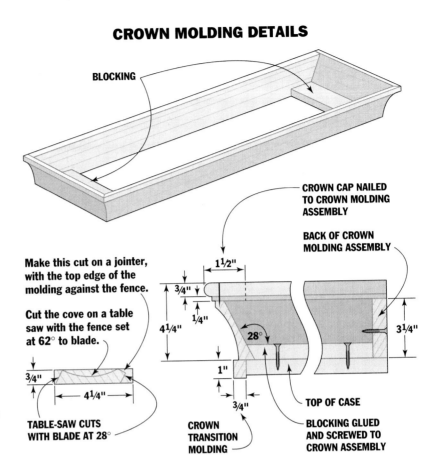

BLOCKING

CROWN CAP NAILED TO CROWN MOLDING ASSEMBLY

BACK OF CROWN MOLDING ASSEMBLY

Make this cut on a jointer, with the top edge of the molding against the fence.

Cut the cove on a table saw with the fence set at 62° to blade.

1½"

¾"

¼"

4¼"

28°

3¼"

1"

¾"

¾"

4¼"

TABLE-SAW CUTS WITH BLADE AT 28°

CROWN TRANSITION MOLDING

TOP OF CASE

BLOCKING GLUED AND SCREWED TO CROWN ASSEMBLY

Photo 5: **Because the top edge of the crown is thin, you'll need to clamp a block of wood to the infeed table to stabilize the workpiece when jointing.**

jointed. Hold the top edge of the molding against the jointer fence, and make a few passes until the width of the flat is about ⅜ inch wide, as shown in **Photo 5** on page 117.

Miter the molding with a chop saw. You need to make a compound cut, but you can do that on a standard chop saw, as shown in **Photo 6.** The molding is cut face out but upside down. The setup would be identical in a tall miter box with a handsaw. The crown sits right on top of the cabinet, like a hat, but you need to assemble it into a frame first—that's where the back of the crown assembly comes in. Cut the ends of the back at a 28-degree angle. Attach the side crown pieces to the back with glue and finish nails first, then glue and nail the front onto the sides. Cut the bottom blocking with a 28-degree angle at the front, and attach it to the crown assembly. Finally, shape the crown-cap molding, using a ¾-inch bull-nose cutter. Miter the crown cap, and nail it to the top edge of the crown. Attach the crown assembly with 1¼-inch screws through the blocking.

9 **Make the shelves.** Pile the shelves face up and with the front edges facing the same way. Draw lines down the front edges of the entire stack to locate the biscuit joints, as shown in **Photo 7.** Cut the biscuit slots in the shelves. Lay the shelf front edges in a row and mark them as you marked the shelves, then cut the slots in one shelf edge at a time. Glue and clamp the edges to all the shelves.

10 **Finish the bookcase.** Sand all the surfaces with medium grit sandpaper—150 grit is sufficient for a painted project. Break all the edges also. Brush or spray on a coat of interior primer, followed by a coat of latex enamel.

Photo 6: To cut the compound miter, attach an auxiliary base and fence to the chop saw. A stop screwed to the base holds the molding at the same angle it will be installed at, only upside down. Make the cuts with the blade set at 45 degrees.

Photo 7: Biscuit joinery usually requires that you mark the location of each biscuit on each workpiece. You can speed the process by marking all the shelves and shelf edges at the same time.

INDEX